# CAPTURING
## the Heart of God

**Pleasing the Father in Everyday Life**

DIANE PARSONS

FOREWORD BY DR. RON KENOLY

Parsons Publishing House
Stafford, Virginia USA

CAPTURING THE HEART OF GOD
by Diane Parsons

Parsons Publishing House
P. O. Box 488
Stafford, VA 22554 USA
www.ParsonsPublishingHouse.com
Info@ParsonsPublishingHouse.com



ISBN -13: 978-1-60273-008-3
ISBN -10: 1602730083
Library of Congress Control Number: 2010908078

Printed in the United States of America.
For World-Wide Distribution.

# TABLE OF CONTENTS

# ACKNOWLEDGEMENTS

Like all of us, I would absolutely be no where without the Lord stepping into my life and making me brand new. He set my feet on a solid rock and gave me a reason for living. Thank You, Lord, for saving my soul.

*I love you, Lord*
*And I lift my voice*
*To worship You,*
*Oh my soul, rejoice.!*
*Take joy, my king*
*In what You hear*
*Let it be a sweet, sweet sound*
*In Your ear.*

"I Love You, Lord" words and music by Laurie Klein

©1978, 1980 House of Mercy Music/Maranatha! Music

Next, I would like to thank my husband, Darrrell Parsons, for his encouragement and ability to draw the best out of me. To Darrell I say: marrying you was the best thing that ever happened to me. You are the love of my life and my best friend. I am so blessed to be your partner in life. The respect and honor that you give me propel me onward and upward. You have changed my life and made me a better person. Your widor and knowledge have increased me in every way. I love you and am grateful for our twenty-four plus years of marriage.

My precious daughter, Brianna, is my joy and helper. Her grammar gift is greatly appreciated and heavily relied upon. To Brianna: You are the best daughter a mother could ever be blessed with. You are fun, yet full of thought. It's exciting to watch you continue to develop your tender heart and sensitivity to God. My prayer for you is that you take the road that God has for your life and find the happiness and great joy that He has for you. Thank you for your encouragement.

I would also like to thank Pastors Ed and Nora King for nurturing me in the Kingdom and my walk with the Lord. I appreciate your investment in my life.

To Dr. and Mrs. Gerald Doggett, I am grateful for your input and influence in my life. Your wisdom is unparalleled. My admonition to you Sis. D is to just keep your eyes open as you pray and look to the future.

To Pastors Robert and Stacey Gay, you have stretched me and increased me in ways I never imagined. I appreciate your integrity, love of the flock and your friendship.

Next, I want to acknowledge Dr. Ron and Tavita Kenoly who have been a wonderful example of Jesus in the earth. I appreciate your friendship and count it a privilege to serve the Lord alongside you.

Finally, to my friends who have encouraged and prayed for me to complete this work which I started twenty-six years ago: Jeanette, Michele, Eva, and many Facebook friends. Thank you.

# FOREWORD

## by Dr. Ron Kenoly

I've known Diane Parsons for over ten years now. We have worked together in ministry serving the body of Christ in many ways. She is not only a great wife to her husband, a fantastic mother to her daughter, and a "Proverbs 31" woman of God, she is also a deep and passionate thinker who is very capable of expressing her thoughts in writing with sensitivity and great attention to detail. I am confident that this book will captivate its readers, inspire and motivate them to greater works and service in the Kingdom of God.

Dr. Ron Kenoly
Worship Leader and Teacher
Ron Kenoly Ministries
Orlando, Florida USA

# ENDORSEMENT

## by Bishop Gerald Doggett

From the beginning of time, children have sought affirmation from their fathers. In this book Diane Parsons provides fresh insights, born from her life experience of pleasing God, which will help each reader embrace the affirmation of our Heavenly Father. This book is a must for every traveler on this journey of life.

Having known Darrell, Diane & Brianna Parsons for many years, I've had the opportunity to observe the wisdom, energy, and core values of an exceptional family. Their attention to detail, and each member walking in Biblical order, has provided a quality example for everyone who has been touched by their life.

Although their personal achievements are too numerous to list in this short writing; I will note one overwhelming quality. While supporting each other in the pursuit of their personal dream, both Darrell and Diane have found the time and joys of watching their daughter, Brianna grow into a gracious young lady with dreams of her own.

Family decisions have always been made with an ear to the mouth of God; and obedience to His command. The content of this book, as well as others they have written, will always reflect the wisdom, character, and strength of a balanced, dedicated life to each other, and to God.

Whether you meet this family personally, or through their publishing company or through a book either of them has written, you will find them a source of strength and inspiration.

Bishop Gerald Doggett
Gerald Doggett Ministries
Apopka, Florida USA

# Introduction

## The Chant of Heaven

The scene is set around the majestic throne of heaven. The players are the twenty-four elders of heaven lying prostrate. As they kneel at the feet of the One sitting on the throne, they begin to chant. The words of the chant go like this: "Thou art worthy, O Lord, to receive glory and honour and power: for thou hast created all things, and for thy pleasure they are and were created (Revelation 4:11, KJV). Another translation records the chant in different words, "Worthy, O Master! Yes, our God! Take the glory! the honor! the power! You created it all; it was created because you wanted it" (MSG). Imagine, this is being sung in heaven now.

You were created to bring pleasure to God. You were created because He wanted you. The God of the Universe wanted you!! The Creator of all things wanted you because it pleased Him – it delighted Him.

This book is a product of my life. I have been studying this topic and writing on this project for over twenty-six years. Over the years as I studied and researched and grew closer to the Lord, I finally realized that capturing God's heart is a life-journey not an eight-week Bible study. Pleasing God with your life begins with making a decision to please Him every minute of every hour of every day. Becoming the delight of the Father is not about being perfect, but having a heart that runs after Him. As I continue on my journey, I invite you to walk with me.

How can we find God's favor? How can we become His delight? How can we capture the heart of God? How can we turn His face towards us?

I challenge you today to discover this purpose in your life. I challenge you to set new sights on your relationship with your Heavenly Father. I admonish you to go forward and seek God's face and His favor. I encourage you to live each day of your life to please the Lord. You don't have to wait for the end of your life to hear God say: "This is My beloved child in whom I am WELL PLEASED." Let's begin our journey today!

The stage is set. The players are in place. Let's join the elders around God's throne and let our voices rise to heaven to give Him glory, honor, and power as we become the delight of the Father!!

To the man who pleases him, God gives wisdom, knowledge and happiness, but to the sinner he gives the task of gathering and storing up wealth to hand it over to the one who pleases God.

Ecclesiastes 2:26, NIV

# Chapter 1

# The Journey of God

## Where Art Thou?

*"And the Lord God called unto Adam and said unto him, where art thou?" (Genesis 3:9, KJV).*

Have you ever felt that God is a million miles away? Have you ever felt like His silence was deafening? On the other hand, as you went about your daily life, have you ever felt He was closer than your very breath? Have you felt God searching for you? Have you ever been wooed by the Holy One into His presence?

In Genesis 1:2 the earth was void and without form and darkness was on the face of the earth. At the same time, melodic praises filled the heavenly Kingdom. Yet, in the midst of all the grandeur of God, pride entered the heart of the third arch angel: Lucifer had fallen and was banned from heaven. The timbrel and the pipes of the anointed cherub were forever silenced (Ezekiel 28). The heavenly hosts were divided; the family was broken. One third of God's angels followed Lucifer's leadership. Acappella praises now filled the corridors of heaven by the remaining angelic forces—Lucifer's music was absent.

Lucifer, the anointed angel, became satan, the accuser. This anointed cherub fell to the earth. Once he was kicked out of heaven, he continued his plan to become equal with God which included separating man from their Creator. Today, the accuser wants you to remain separated from God. In the Garden of Eden, the evil satan seemed victorious at first, but God... God had another plan.

As I have sought the Lord over the years, one of my favorite verses has become 2 Chronicles 16:9 which says, "For the eyes of the LORD move to and fro throughout the earth that He may strongly support those whose heart is completely His" (NASB). God is always watching... always searching. He's looking and watching. A different flavor of this verse can be found in another translation: "For the eyes of the LORD run to and fro throughout the whole earth, to show Himself strong on behalf of those whose heart is loyal to Him" (NKJV). In giving Him your whole heart, you show your loyalty to Him. God is looking to show Himself big and strong on your behalf... as long as your heart is completely His—as long as you are sold out to Him!! The Lord God began a search. For whom was and is He searching? The eyes of the Lord move to and fro throughout the earth SEARCHING... always searching for those whose hearts are completely His.

Sin entered the world through satan, but it entered mankind through Adam. Once Adam sinned, God formulated a plan to restore His family. The great Bible teacher and pastor Dr. E. W. Kenyon wrote a book entitled ***The***

***Father and His Family*** which brings insight and revelation to this subject. God began looking for you. He patiently set the stage to embrace sinful man and receive His family once again unto Himself. Once sin entered, a new man would have to become the "redeemed of the Lord"—but this plan would take thousands of years to be known in the earth. God had you in mind as He begins His journey.

## The Journey

The journey starts in a garden east of Eden. Eden translates in Hebrew as "delight." The fullness of God's delight was displayed and expressed in this garden. God was pleased with His creation and it was very good.

God placed His small family in the garden of His delight. The Lord commanded Adam and Eve to be fruitful, multiply, and replenish the earth. Through satan's influence, treachery, sin, faithlessness, and disobedience soon entered their hearts and distanced the Father from His family. Not long into man's journey, God became disappointed with His creation. It is recorded, "And the LORD was sorry that He had made man on the earth, and He was grieved in His heart" (Genesis 6:6, NKJV).

Man's sin had separated him from God; mankind had to be restored or recovered back from that sin. Since the Lord can have no part in sin, fellowship between God and man was broken. However, righteous Noah found favor in God's eyes as he walked with God and became a partner in God's covenant (*see* Genesis 6). The great flood erased mankind with the exception of Noah and his family and the Lord began His plan anew. Old things were new. At this point, the Eternal Father set the stage to start a family through the bloodline of his favored Noah.

He looked across time to thousands of years in the future and saw the Promise of His Son—the Messiah, Jesus the Christ—coming to Earth to once again unite God and man. In the presence of the Lord, a day is as a thousand years and a thousand years is as a day. Time is different in His kingdom; God transcends or works outside of our timeline. What may seem a lifetime to change is only a moment in His presence. As your journey begins and all along the way, mistakes and problems of the past can be removed and cast into the sea of forgetfulness never again to be remembered. Never again will our regrets be used against us by satan, the accuser.

Depending on the blood of bulls and goats to cover man's sin, God's journey continued between the two cherubim on the ark to commune with His people. Each step of this journey was a masterfully crafted part of the grand scheme for the redemption of mankind. Each step of this journey was revealed through a new covenant with man. The overture of God's love was intertwined with His every word, every thought and every deed. Through the years, His search continued.

He called out from a bush to a man named Abraham who ventured to believe Him. Father Abraham's only qualifications seemed simple: he believed God and he would teach his children about *Jehovah Jireh*, the provider.

God looked onward into the future and again came into another agreement with the Israelites, His chosen people. However, there had to be insulation between a holy God and man to cover the sin of Adam which was passed through the bloodline to future generations. There were cleansings and offerings which were made because sinful man could not fellowship with a sinless God. The blood of bulls and goats covered the sin of man for yet another year. Fellowship with God resumed only through the mediation of priests. Deuteronomy records the testimony of this covenant with Israel/Jacob:

> He found him (Israel) in a desert land and in the vast howling wilderness; he led him, he instructed him, he kept him as the apple of his eye. As an eagle stirreth up her nest, fluttereth over her young, spreadeth abroad her wings, taketh them, beareth them on her wings: So the LORD alone did lead him, and there was no strange god with him. (Deuteronomy 32:10-12, KJV).

The next covenant that followed was with Moses who bore the reflection of God's glory and led His people; he understood God's ways – not just His acts as did the children of Israel (*see* Psalm 103:7). There is a place we can live in God above the history of His acts and learn His ways. You may know facts about your favorite preacher or movie star, but you don't "know" them. You know someone by understanding how they think and how they respond to things. You can know God like this. Moses found grace in the sight of the Lord and God tenderly showed the man of flesh the hinder parts of His glory in a rare interaction between God and man (*see* Exodus 33). God entrusted this man to record His Law until the Promised Messiah could enter the scene and then the law would be written upon the human heart.

We continue down the hallowed halls of human history and find another notable man and another notable covenant. King David was found to be the apple of God's eye (1 Samuel 13:14, Psalm 17:8) and a man after God's own heart (Acts 13:22). God affirmed His covenant with man once again through David's son, Solomon, for an eternal Kingdom among the peoples of the earth. Solomon was favored and granted the privilege of building God's house.

When we look ahead a couple of millennia we see Jesus. The stage had been set and the players were in place. The journey of God culminated as the Promised Messiah was born into the earth. The Son of *Elohim*, the Almighty God, was clothed in flesh with divine blood flowing through His veins (Philippians 2:7). Immortality put on mortality. The Son of God hung up the glory of the heavenly Kingdom and came into the earth – a kingdom of sin, dirt, and decay. The culmination of God's plan was manifested in the birth, death, and resurrection of Jesus Christ. The final covenant – the New Covenant – fulfilled the Law. The only begotten Son of God became the first born of many brethren and He became the first born from the dead. The plan of God was fulfilled and we were all given entrance to His family by grace through faith in what Jesus had accomplished. The Lord now had a family.

## The Completed Work

God began a search when the earth was void and without form. His search was for sons and daughters who had a heart completely and totally dedicated to Him. When sin entered the world, it separated man from God. The perfect, sinless God could no longer fellowship with His creation. God determined to draw His family back to Himself through a trail of historic covenants with man.

Through the birth, life, sacrifice, and resurrection of Jesus Christ, the heavenly veil separating the holy God from sinful man was eradicated. At the same time, Mark records this observation, "And the veil of the temple was rent in twain from the top to the bottom" (Mark 15:38, KJV). It was torn in half. The literal veil in the Jerusalem temple is reported to have been four inches thick and weighed about four tons requiring three hundred men to hold it. It was literally torn from top to bottom as only God could tear it. Something supernatural definitely took place. When we come into God's family through Jesus Christ, the spiritual veil between God and man is no more. There is a wonderful song by Dean Mitchum called "The Veil is Gone" and the lyrics are: The Veil is gone, no partition, no hidden thing, no separation. What a great truth! A simple prayer of salvation and repentance from dead works will make you a partaker of the completed work of Jesus, the Anointed One. We have a new destiny and we have access to the Father once again.

## For What Was God Searching?

British educator and author, Thomas Arnold (1795-1842) once said, "The distinction between Christianity and all other systems of religion consists largely in this, that in these others, men are found seeking after God, while Christianity is God seeking after men." God is searching for you!

Now that you and I have entrance to the Father through Jesus Christ, is the heart of God satisfied and content? I venture to say that God is continually seeking for those whose hearts are daily committed to Him. I think we would all agree that there is a difference between a Christian life with "hell insurance" and a Christian life which is wholly devoted to the King of Kings and Lord of Lords – a vessel fit for the Master's use. Again, I'm not talking about living in perfection; I'm talking about living with a heart toward God.

I love this verse so much that I'm going to quote it again: 2 Chronicles 16:9 says, "The eyes of the Lord search to and fro throughout the earth searching for those whose heart is completely His." He searches for our hearts, not our spotless lives. God, who knows our heart, has already told us that no one is perfect. We read in 1 John 1:8, "If we say that we have no sin, we deceive ourselves, and the truth is not in us (KJV)." However, God has provided a remedy. We read in the Word that when we sin, He is faithful and just to forgive us and cleanse us of that sin. God is not looking for perfection. He's looking for your heart. If He has your heart, He can mold and shape you into His image.

**ACTION POINT: Let us pray that our heart becomes His heart.**

If you want to get God's attention, begin your revolutionary journey now in capturing His heart and being well-pleasing to Him. It is a journey on your way to your eternal destiny. This road will bring fulfillment to every aspect of your life and will culminate when we see Him face to face. Let's start this journey together now.

# Chapter 2

# Why Were We Created?

## And for Thy Pleasure...

If you're on a search to find why you exist on this earth—you have picked up the right book. If you're trying to find your purpose—continue to read with me.

Why were we created? What is the goal of our life? Answers to these questions have been sought for millennia. These questions of the ages have answers that can be found in the Word of God—the Holy Bible. The indisputable Word of God says, "...for thy pleasure they are and were created (Revelation 4:11, KJV)." We were created to bring pleasure and delight to our Heavenly Father. It's a fact for today and tomorrow—a simple truth! You may be saying, "That sounds huge. How can I do that?" Just as your earthly parents may have done in your life, God has not been silent about what He likes and does not like. He has revealed Himself through His Word.

Our Heavenly Father is gathering together a family. The blood of Jesus cleanses us from sin and allows us to enter the family of God. This family is not a group of religious zealots or faith fanatics or perfect people in their own flesh. There's a lot of truth in the bumper sticker seen on cars: Christians aren't perfect—just forgiven. There may be a wide variety of reasons why someone would put that on their vehicle, but it doesn't negate the truth in the statement.

The family of God is a gathering of individuals who have made Jesus their Lord and have as a single goal to celebrate their Father and bring Him joy as we do His works. As we do the specific tasks He's called us to perform in this life and keep our heart focused on pleasing Him, we will be successful. Everything in our lives should be all about our great God—a great Father. Our life is all about CAPTURING THE HEART OF GOD and becoming His delight.

Enoch's testimony was that he pleased God (Hebrews 11:5). This is our choice. Let us set our face like flint to become well-pleasing to God and the delight of our Father.

### Your Purpose

In 1963, Pauline Michael Mills penned a song entitled, "Thou Art Worthy." That song was re-recorded in 1975 and became a standard in church repertoires all over the world. One line of the lyrics says, "...and for thy pleasure, they were created. Thou Art Worthy O Lord." That line is straight out of the Bible. I sang that song for years and never allowed the truth of that Scripture to enter my heart and change me. I—a simple girl from Tennessee—was formed in my mother's womb to be a delight to the King of

Kings and Lord of Lords—the Mighty God—the great I AM. You were created for that purpose, too!

You may be struggling about who you are and what you are supposed to do in this life. Stop and rest in this truth: you were born on this earth at this time to bring pleasure to the Creator of the Universe.

## Learning to Please God

As a new Christian, I was ignorant about God. I began to seek the Lord, and He showed me that I could actually know Him—intimately—by reading His Word. I saw how Moses knew the ways of God where the children of Israel only knew His acts. At that point, I began to soak myself in the Bible to learn the ways of God.

We find the perfect will of God from reading and understanding His Word. Knowledge of the Bible will keep you free from the bondage of sin.

As we continue to read and commit to act on the Word, the Teacher of the Church, the Holy Spirit (Luke 12:12), will teach you how to bring delight to your heavenly Father and how to capture His heart. God does not leave us in the dark about what He likes and does not like. It has been revealed! Paul writes in 1 Thessalonians 4:2, "As you have learned from us the way of life that pleases God" (Phillips). The goal of the covenants of God, as shown in the Old and New Testaments, is to reveal the way for us to please our Heavenly Father.

The full pleasure of God is culminated and demonstrated in the life of Jesus, the Christ. As we read about the life of the precious Son of God, we see an example of a life that is pleasing to the Lord. Jesus' testimony in His own words is, "I always do those things that please him (John 8:29)." Let us pray that we might do the same.

**ACTION POINT: Let us pray that we might always do the things that please our Father God.**

## Chapter 3

# Matters of the Heart

When I was nineteen I began to sense God wooing me into His Kingdom. It was in my early Christian years that I heard some preachers say, "God is no respecter of persons. We are all the same in God's eyes." The Bible does say that God is not a respecter of persons, but what does that mean? You cannot possibly read the Bible and conclude that God treats everyone the same. You really can't conclude this statement either, "If He did it for me, He'll do it for you." What? This may be a person's attempt to say, "Hey, I'm not special." But, on the other hand, let's don't give crazy hope to a person. Look at His love for David and His mercy for Solomon and His anger towards King Saul. It is more accurate to say that God treats right hearts the same. For all of those who capture His heart with a single-focused devotion, God does treat them the same; He pours out His blessings on them and grants them His favor.

As I read, I saw God interacting with the man Adam when they walked in the cool of the day and fellowshipped in the garden. I saw God favor Abraham as a man trustworthy to teach his children about the Lord *Jehovah* and His covenants. The shepherd named Moses was commanded by God to the mountaintop and it was there that Moses viewed God's back and witnessed the finger of God writing the Ten Commandments. Moses made Himself available to be used by God—whether he felt confident about it or not.

David, the simple shepherd boy, who was chosen to be King, dared to believe God. He was a young, ruddy kid that was available to be used by the King of Kings for His purposes. An old adage states that it's not our ability that God looks for, it's our availability. David became the apple of God's eye through his devotion and sincerity of heart. King David was not favored because of his perfection and sinless life—far from it; however, his willingness to repent and his love for his Lord brought God's favor in return. Once God had David's heart, He could enforce a change in his behavior; David was pliable in God's hands.

Over and over again, I saw in the Bible that God does not treat us all alike. God offers His Kingdom to all, but only those who accept Him can enter into eternal life. God offers His favor to all, but only those who accept this intimacy will walk in it.

## Spanish Class

My daughter has a Spanish teacher who appreciates the fact that my daughter really puts a lot of effort into her studies. On test essay questions, my daughter will write two times the amount expected because she loves Spanish and she loves doing it. Her teacher responded by giving Brianna extra credit because of all the extra effort she puts in her answers. I would say that the teacher likes all of her students, and I would also say that if every student would give the teacher more than expected, they, too, would receive extra credit. Does the teacher like my daughter more than the other kids? No, I would say that she is rewarding or favoring her. Is Senora Rivera rewarding Brianna because my daughter likes Spanish? No. Is she favoring Brianna because she does what's expected? No, a lot of kids are doing what is expected of them. Is she rewarding Brianna because she's a beautiful, young lady? No, the classroom is full of them. She favors Brianna with extra credit because Brianna did what was expected of her ***and then doubled it***; she gave her teacher much more than her teacher ever expected. Brianna's interest and devotion were pleasing to her Spanish teacher.

Senora Rivera's response is a natural human response; she awarded Brianna extra credit—credit given above the norm. Is Brianna special? To me she is, but I would venture to say that Senora Rivera has had many kids like my daughter come her way. I would also venture to say that any child in that class—in any of this teacher's classes—who goes above and beyond the average expectations, will receive that same favor or same blessing. The smiley face that her teacher draws on her test papers shows that her teacher is pleased with Brianna's work; it makes the teacher happy to instill a love for the language and an excellent skill level in a student. Is Senora Rivera partial to my daughter? No, I think she sees the same excitement in Brianna that the teacher herself feels and she rewards the extra effort that is spawned out of that love for the language. The result for my daughter is a better grade and an encouragement to continue to excel and push further into the language. That favor draws her to be like her teacher. That favor draws her further to be her best and do her best—plus she gets a better grade in the here and now.

God is a lot like this. He rewards us as we strive to be like Him. He pours out His favor on us which draws us closer to Him. Our blessings are not just reserved for heaven; we are blessed in the here and now.

### At Home

A parent's responsibility is to teach your child how to behave in your household and in life. You have the expectation that they are going to do as you instructed. When they do what they are told you are satisfied and glad. When they do it without you having to ask them it brings great pleasure; you feel that they are really maturing. It shows that what's important to you has now become important to them. If you walked into your child's room and they had cleaned it without you asking, it would most likely bring a big smile to your face. I know I certainly appreciate it. The Lord appreciates it when His heart becomes our heart; His desires become our desires. We capture His heart when He sees us doing the things that are important to Him and acting like Him.

**ACTION POINT: Let's make decisions that will put a smile on God's face.**

### Apple of God's Eye

We have discussed how David was a man after God's own heart and that he was the apple of God's eye. Do you want to be the apple of God's eye? In Psalm 119:58, David reminds the Lord, "I entreated Your favor with my whole heart;" (NKJV). David messed up a lot, but he went after God with his whole heart. If God has our heart, He can help us with the rest.

The Bible says that God is not a respecter of persons—of their personhood; however, He is a respecter of hearts. If He is a respecter of hearts, then we, too, can find a place of delight in God if we allow our hearts to be conformed to the Lord. The entire Bible records the real-life events of people who walked on this earth. These life stories are to be our examples. 1 Corinthians 10:11, reads, "Now all these things happened to them as examples, and they were written for our admonition" (NKJV). The people in the Bible were not perfect, but their lives are recorded so we can do what they did to get positive results and avoid what they did which netted negative results.

## No Partial Payment

Let's get back to the point of God not being a respecter of persons. You find that truth restated in Acts 10:34-35 which records, "Then Peter opened his mouth, and said, Of a truth I perceive that God is no respecter of persons: But in every nation he that feareth him, and worketh righteousness, is accepted with him" (KJV). What does this Scripture mean? One cannot understand this Scripture without reading past the colon found in Acts 10:34. The colon represents the point where the thought is explained. Let us move past this colon and choose to live by the whole truth of the Bible!

The setting of this verse is that Peter is receiving the revelation that the Gospel is for everyone. God's call to salvation goes out to every tongue, tribe, and nation. The more modern New King James Version of this verse says, "In truth I perceive that God shows no partiality. But in every nation whoever fears Him and works righteousness is accepted by Him." Does this mean that God treats us all the same? As you read through the Holy Writ, do you see that God responds the same way to all of the Bible heroes & heroines? No, I don't. This verse is saying that He is no longer just the God of the Jews; He has made His Kingdom available to us all. The Gentiles can now come into covenant with God. I see a God who does not look at race, ethnicity, or gender. I see a God who does look at the heart of those who reverence Him and rely on His completed work, and He rewards those with His favor.

As we take an in-depth look at this verse, we see the Greek words for "no respecter of persons" are translated as "one who exhibits partiality." What is "partiality"? There are three commonly used definitions for this word. The very first definition listed in a standard dictionary of the English language says that "partiality" is, "the state of being partial." Let's not stop here. What is being "partial?" The definition of this adjective "partial" is "of, relating to, being or affecting only a part, not total, incomplete." God does not half do things. The plan of salvation is completed. He is the author and finisher of our faith! God doesn't just save **some** who call on Him, He saves **all** who call on Him. If you accept Jesus as your personal Lord, He will save you regardless of your demographics.

These definitions only confirm what Luke explained after the colon in this verse. Let's look at the verse again.

Acts 10:34-35 says, "Then Peter opened his mouth, and said, Of a truth I perceive that God is no respecter of persons: But in every nation he that feareth him, and worketh righteousness, is accepted with him" (KJV). Luke recorded here what Peter preached following the Day of Pentecost. The revelation given was that the truth of Scripture was not only for the Jews, but for the Gentiles, too. After this statement, the Holy Spirit fell on all that heard the Word. Luke also records, "And they of the circumcision which believed were astonished, as many as came with Peter, because that on the Gentiles also was poured out the gift of the Holy Ghost (Acts 10:45, KJV)." Jesus did not just save part of mankind, but He died for all to enter the family of God. The work of Jesus was not partial; He completed His work. Jesus redeemed mankind – not just the Jew, but the Gentile, too.

## Other Testimonies

Does God treat us all the same? What attracted God to Enoch? Was it the fact that Enoch chose to walk with God? Noah received the Lord's attention because of His righteousness. Abraham chose to believe God. King David made mistake after mistake; however, there was something in him that was awarded God's blessing. What was it? The Lord did not even treat David and Solomon the same. Obviously, God does not treat us all the same. If not, then how do we become His delight? How do we obtain His favor?

## Obtaining God's Favor

Jesus came to save individuals. He wants to be your personal Lord and Savior. A much quoted truth attributed to many different people says, "God has no grandchildren." We all must enter the Kingdom of God for ourselves—not on the coat-tail of your spouse or your family or your church or even your citizenship. Jesus wants to be your Lord and He must have permission to enter into your life.

Since we come to Jesus as an individual, He deals with us as individuals. The world does not want to recognize that God is God. If they do acknowledge God, they strive to depersonalize Him. They say IF He exists, He is an entity far, far away and has too much to do to be concerned with a single individual on the earth. The truth of the matter is that God is a God of individuals. The God of the Old Testament used individuals; we are well acquainted with the lives of Adam, Noah, Moses, and David. Several millennia later, Jesus, the Son of God, was born into the earth and He consistently worked through individuals: Matthew, Mark, Paul, and Timothy. Throughout the Bible, it speaks of God knowing our hearts, caring about our needs, and hearing our prayers—not as corporate humanity, but as an individual seeking His God.

The entire Bible records events revolving around men and women who were willing to believe God. How do we rationalize that David was the apple of God's eye, but others were not? We see the great love the Father had for Jesus and how Jesus chose to do the things that pleased God, but others did not. The testimony of Jesus evoked a statement from God that can revolutionize our thinking. The Heavenly Father spoke from heaven and said, "You are My beloved Son; in You I am well pleased" (Luke 3:22, NKJV).

We can become well-pleasing to the Lord. The Bible tells us that there are things that please God and there are things that do not please God—some are actions—some are attitudes of the heart. Bible scholars might say that there are acts of omission (things or feelings that you omit or leave out of your life) and acts of commission (things you do, say, or feel in your life). The prophet Isaiah records the Word of the Lord and God's heart cry, "When I called, no one answered, When I spoke they did not hear; But they did evil before My eyes, And chose that in which I do not delight" (Isaiah 66:4, NKJV). We can choose to bring Him pleasure or not. King David's choice was clear—through all of his imperfections, the cry of his heart was, "I delight to do Your will, O my God" (Psalm 40:8, NKJV). Let that be our heart cry, too.

**ACTION POINT: Let us delight to do God's will.**

We are not Jesus and we are not perfect, but is it possible for you and I to receive the same commendation as Jesus received? We can live our lives and hear, 'this is my beloved child in whom I am well-pleased.' I believe that all Christians should live their lives to that end. Once we become Christians, the Father sees us through the blood of Jesus. He does not see all our imperfections because our mediator cleanses us. You are righteous because Jesus made you righteous. Some people bemoan, "I just don't feel worthy." Well, you're not—not of yourself! No one is worthy to enter heaven. No one is worthy of His blessing. No one is worthy of His favor. We are an unworthy people. However, the truth is that Jesus Christ exchanged our sin for His right standing with God and made us worthy. "For He made Him who knew no sin to be sin for us, that we might become the righteousness of God in Him (2 Corinthians 5:21, NKJV). Jesus put us in right standing with God. The Lord wants us to stand up and believe His Word and accept His covenant! With Jesus, I am worthy! Thank God that we're not left to ourselves.

We don't deserve heaven, but He has given it to us anyway. The Lord offers family benefits! He is a merciful God, and He is faithful and just to forgive us and cleanse us from all of our imperfections and sin. When you talk about this glorious grace, you always have people who take it as a license to sin. Even in Bible days, Paul had to ask if we should sin big so that the grace of God could abound. He answered himself by saying, "God forbid!" Later, we will examine the favor of God and holy living more closely.

**ACTION POINT: Let us pray that we will become aware of Jesus' perfect work of putting us in right standing with the Father.**

# Chapter 4

## Putting First Things First

If you want to live a life that is pleasing to God, you must first belong to His family. Have you ever asked Jesus Christ to come into your heart and be your Lord and Savior—Master, Owner and Ruler? If you have, praise God! You have chosen a life's journey where your testimony can be that you were pleasing to God! If you have not yet accepted Jesus as your Lord, read on.

The Gospel message is good news; God is not angry with you. He's not a big God in heaven holding a hammer ready to whack you at any time you mess up. This is not like the arcade game Whac-A-Mole. The Good News is that God has reconciled—bought back—man to God. We have been brought back to the Creator of the Universe. Adam lost the relationship between God and man, but Jesus regained it. Through His stainless blood shed at Calvary, Jesus paid the price for our sin. Jesus brought together once again the hand of God and the hand of man. The gateway into the family of God has been restored

Are all humans part of the family of God? No, some men have the devil as their father. John 8:44 says, "You are of your father the devil, and the desires of your father you want to do" (NKJV). That means that they wanted to act like the devil. Does being born into a Christian family make one a Christian? No! There's a funny saying that says, "Standing in a garage doesn't make you a car any more than going to church makes you a Christian." That's really true; God has no grandchildren. Every person who comes to God must come to Him on their own.

How do you become part of the family of God? What do you do now? It's not difficult; it's free, but it's not cheap. Jesus did a lot to buy us back from satan's hold. There's a simple way to explain the plan of salvation called the Roman Road. Don't wait! If you have never made Jesus your Lord, walk down this road with me now.

- ALL HAVE SINNED - Romans 3:23, "For all have sinned, and come short of the glory of God" (KJV). We've all messed up; you can't measure up to God.
- EVEN THOUGH YOU WERE A SINNER, JESUS DIED FOR YOU - Romans 5:8 "...while we were yet sinners, Christ died for us" (KJV). Jesus did this before you were living right.
- THE PAYDAY FOR BEING A SINNER IS DEATH; THAT'S WHAT WE'VE EARNED - Romans 6:23, "For the wages of sin is death..." (KJV).
- HOWEVER, GOD OFFERS US A FREE GIFT - Romans 6:23 says, "...the gift of God is eternal life through Jesus Christ our Lord" (KJV). When you get a gift, you must either accept it or reject it.
- BELIEVE WITH YOUR HEART & SPEAK WITH YOUR MOUTH -

Romans 10:10, "For with the heart man believeth unto righteousness; and with the mouth confession is made unto salvation" (KJV).

- If you call on God, You will be saved. It's a promise! - Romans 10:13, "For whosoever shall call upon the name of the Lord shall be saved" (KJV).
- It's by faith! - Romans 4:16 says, "Therefore it is of faith, that it might be by grace..." (KJV) You might not feel different at first, but you will become different.

The prayer of salvation has no official words—you can pray your own words or the words of another—the key thing is that you mean it with all of your heart. You can stand or sit; eyes can be opened or closed. Christianity is a relationship—not a religion. You can pray something like this:

> *"Lord, I come to You in Jesus' name. I recognize that I am a sinner. I also recognize that I need You. Please, come into my life and be my Lord. Save me and deliver me from sin. I want to serve You all the days of my life. Make me like You so I can show Your love to others. I thank you that I am a Christian; I am a member of the family of God. Thank you."*

If you took the time to pray that prayer, you need to tell someone about it. There's a spiritual principle at work here. Matthew 10:32 says, "Whoever acknowledges me before men, I will also acknowledge him before my Father in heaven" (NIV). Tell someone in your life or write/text/email me and let me know.

## Now That You're A Christian

The Bible says that when we first become Christians, we are like little babies. In order to grow spiritually, we need to read an easy-to-understand Bible and join a great local church that teaches the Word of God.

I want to share some truths with you that would have helped me when I first became a Christian. I was a total blank slate in my knowledge about Christianity—you may be, too. Here are a few things that you need to understand about your new family:

First, there is no lack in the Kingdom. You don't ever have to feel that you're in competition with your new family members. God has enough love, blessing, and favor for us all. If the Lord blesses your brother, He still has enough to bless you, too. If we are mindful of this, we can keep jealously and covetousness out of our hearts. There should never be any competition in the family. Remember, we serve *El Shaddai*—the God who's more than enough.

Secondly, develop an attitude of gratitude. Once you realize the tremendous price that was paid for your salvation, you should have no trouble being grateful and appreciative to the Lord.

Thirdly, a family member in good standing will produce good fruit. Do good works and become like your Father. We go into detail on this throughout the remainder of this book.

Fourthly, develop good habits of prayer, Bible reading, and worship. These things will keep you connected to your heavenly Father. Get involved in a strong local church that teaches the Word of God.

Fifthly, God looks on the heart and it is He alone who can judge thoughts and intentions. There is no spiritual gift of suspicion and no spiritual fruit of criticalness. You are not allowed the privilege of judging your brother's heart—just his fruit. We are told to be more concerned about what we need to fix in our own lives and leave other people's shortcomings between them and the Lord (Luke 6:42).

Another thing is that God's ways are not our ways; His ways are above ours. Not everything that the Lord does will make sense to our natural minds. Realize now that this Kingdom operates in the spirit. You won't have good results in your new family if you try to operate in the flesh. However, there is a time to put feet to your prayers and GO into all the world.

Also, when you sin, run **to** God **not** from Him. He is waiting with forgiveness and will make you clean. His mercy is new every morning. As you have a heart for God, you need to repent or turn from sin. He is faithful and just to forgive us. Remember that the blood of Jesus is eternal. His blood didn't just cleanse us when we first prayed, but it continues to cleanse us.

Next, when you come to God with your whole heart, you are in His family; He will never leave you or forsake you. However, just as you voluntarily came into the family, you can voluntarily leave it, too. If you decide that you don't want to be a Christian, God has given you the sovereign will to make that decision. Jesus said, "No one, having put his hand to the plow, and looking back, is fit for the kingdom of

God" (Luke 9:62). The Apostle Peter tells you that God will let you out if you want out (2 Peter 2:20-21). Perfection didn't get you into the Kingdom and a lack of perfection won't get you out; however, you need to keep your heart towards God and repent of all wrong doing. Don't allow your heart to be hardened to sin. A wonderful minister, Dr. Roy Hicks said, "Sin will take me farther than I want to go; keep me longer than I want to stay; cost me more than I can pay." Unconfessed & unrepented of sin will lead you down the ultimate road of turning from God.

Finally and most importantly, walk in love. Walk in love. Walk in love. Since God is love, when you walk in love, you're acting like your heavenly Father. Study 1 Corinthians 13 and find out about real love—not the world's idea of love. Love does not get offended and it is not rude. It doesn't think just about itself. Love doesn't get all puffed up with pride. Love is kind and patient. It thinks the best about others. Love "bears all things, believes all things, hopes all things, endures all things" (1 Corinthians 13:7).

Welcome to the family! Now, we are all able to continue together in our journey to become the delight of the Father. Let's move on.

# Chapter 5

## It's Your Choice

God created man with a free will. He desired a family that would choose Him—not be forced into relationship with Him. Freely God gives His love and He wants to receive it back freely. The Lord wants to give His family an excitement about tomorrow and a passion for life today. In Jeremiah 29:11 God tells us, "For I know the thoughts that I think toward you, says the LORD, thoughts of peace and not of evil, to give you a future and a hope." God is good and He has good thoughts towards us! In this day of hopelessness, the Lord has given us hope. In this day of fear about tomorrow, He has given us a future. Heaven is our ultimate future, but God has a good future for us here on the earth, too.

Life, from the Greek word *zoe* which means *the God-kind of life*, comes to those who make wise decisions. God gives us the choice to serve Him. Heaven or hell. Life or death. Blessing or cursing. We have a choice. The Bible removes all doubt and tells us precisely how to choose life:

love Him, obey Him, and cling to Him. Deuteronomy 30:19-20 says:

> I call heaven and earth as witnesses today against you, that I have set before you life and death, blessing and cursing; therefore choose life, that both you and your descendants may live; that you may love the LORD your God, that you may obey His voice, and that you may cling to Him, for He is your life and the length of your days.

The result of loving, obeying, and clinging to God is LIFE! The result of not loving, not obeying, and not clinging is death. The life we speak of is not breathing and the death we speak of is not the cessation of breathing. The *God-kind of life* is when we exist in God's presence and where death is eternal separation from Him. Jesus defeated death for the Christian and we will spend eternity with our heavenly Father.

How do we walk out our choice of life each day? We demonstrate our love, obedience and clinging to God with our tongue. We see in Proverbs 18:21 that, "Death and life are in the power of the tongue" (NKJV). Our choice for death or life can be evidenced through the words we speak or sing. This is why praise and worship is so important to the believer. It is recorded that our sacrifice of praise is the "fruit of our lips, giving thanks to His name" (Hebrews 13:15). With our words, we may choose to build up or tear down. When we choose life, we build up. We are imitating Jesus when we choose to build up. Words of death always tear down. The devil comes to steal, kill, and destroy, but Jesus came to give abundant life.

We are to live our lives to bring pleasure to the Father God. Apparently, God is none too happy when we choose to do those things that are not pleasing. Thank the Lord for His forgiveness when we mess up; we are to run to Him when we err—not away from Him. We must rely on God's forgiveness when we sin. This verse should be the foundation of our Christian walk, "If we confess our sins, He is faithful and just to forgive us our sins and to cleanse us from all unrighteousness" (1 John 1:9). He doesn't just forgive; He cleanses us from it, too! Our sins may be as scarlet, but Jesus washes them white as snow. Our sin is not too big for God to forgive and cleanse.

The things that are not pleasing to God are evil. Let us continually commit to do only those things which are pleasing to God.

**ACTION POINT: Choose to be a builder in every area of your life. Be a people builder!**

## How to Walk

We discussed earlier that we have the privilege to make choices in our lives. God is not interested in us being like robots; He is interested in His family. After we choose life by making Jesus our Lord and Saviour, we need to learn how to live this new life. We need to learn how to walk pleasing to Him.

Salvation is the beginning of life, not the end of it. Too many Christians walk an aisle or pray a prayer and never allow the King of Kings to change them. It is as if they say to the Lord, "Come, but don't come too close. Save me, but don't change me." Some want to remain Sunday morning Christians; however, we said earlier that God does not do things halfway. He does not half save us and He does not want just half of our heart. He searches the world over for those who will give their whole heart completely to Him. If you are reading this book now, you are probably not numbered among the half-hearted. You obviously have or are looking for a deeper relationship with the Lord.

Enoch's testimony is that he walked with God. How can we do that today? If we walk with God, we must know Him. We covered salvation earlier, but I'm talking about an intimate knowing of our Heavenly Father. When I was born-again at nineteen years old, I was an ignorant young college student. I didn't know anything about the Bible. I just knew that I had never been saved and I was compelled that I needed to do that—whatever that meant. After I prayed the prayer of salvation, the Lord wooed me to Himself. I remember crying out to God with tears streaming down my cheeks, "Lord, how can I know you?" At that moment, the God of the universe spoke to my heart clearly and vividly—and firmly. He said, "Read My Word." It was a clear and simple answer. I began the quest of a lifetime. I hungered and thirsted for His Word. I consumed the Bible at the university I was attending—between classes, in the library, on the bus, in the parking lot. I read the Bible at home—during television commercials, between studying, late at night and early in the morning. The Lord showed me the key to knowing Him was to know Him through the Word of God. He showed me His ways. I could see how He thought, what was important to Him, and understand His modus operandi—the way He operated.

The people at your work or school may know your history—your past jobs or your previous schooling; however, your spouse or your best friend is going to understand what makes you tick; they understand your motives and your intentions. They know your disappointments and your dreams. You have revealed your heart to those you trust and hold dear. God revealed Himself in a special way to His servant Moses. I want to reiterate here: the children of Israel knew God's acts, but Moses knew His ways. The Israelites could recite the historical actions of *Jehovah* God and sing it in three-part harmony, but Moses understood and knew His heart.

**ACTION POINT: Let us set our face to know God's ways.**

The Bible is a love letter from the Father to His children. By reading the Bible, we can know God's ways. Once we know God's ways, we can understand how to walk in order to please Him. The Apostle Paul had one goal when writing letters to the various churches. He summarized what the Thessalonians received from him, "...you have learned from us the way of life that pleases God" (1 Thessalonians 4:1, Phillips). Let us make a commitment to read and absorb God's Word so that we may learn to please our heavenly Father.

# Chapter 6

# What Is Delight?

## The Will of God

In the Garden of Eden, God gave man the responsibility to be fruitful on the earth, replenish the earth, and subdue it. The Lord gave the same task to Noah after the flood. That commission for mankind has never changed. As a matter of fact, in 1 Corinthians 15:45 Jesus is referred to as the last Adam which would also encompass that responsibility. The responsibility for us to be fruitful, replenish, and subdue the earth is still in effect today.

If you ever have a question about what God's will is, read the Bible. We have two testaments—or covenants —of God's Word in our Bible. As a lawyer discusses a person's "will and testament," we can also refer to the Bible as the will of God. The old contract was fulfilled in the life, death, and resurrection of Jesus Christ. We continue to live under the new contract today. The truth and principles demonstrated and taught in the Old and New Testaments show us God's will.

What is God's will? Let us disregard all of the religious connotations. His will for us is to obey Him out of a willing heart. Our job is to do what He said. It's so much nicer when our kids willingly obey us; we can force them to do things, but oh what a blessing when they do it gladly. I used to remind my daughter, "All I want you to do is o-b-e-y! All God wants you to do is o-b-e-y." That is God's simple direction: obey from a willing heart. It's not hard or complicated. Sometimes a rebellious nature rises up to reject God's simple command. We try to twist it around and get it confused, but God wants us to obey. What has He told all of us to do in His Word? To name a few, He has told us to love Him, be fruitful, replenish the earth, subdue the earth, and love our neighbors as ourselves. The summation of the Bible is: love the Lord your God with all your heart, soul, and mind and love your neighbor as yourself. The wonderful thing about God is that He says to obey Him and then He says, 'I know it's hard to obey so I'll give you power to obey Me.' He gave us the Helper – the Holy Spirit – to help us live a life that's pleasing to Him.

It should be our desire to please God. It should be a Christian's natural inclination to perform God's will—not natural in the flesh, but natural to the re-born spirit. We are encouraged in the Scriptures, along with John the Baptist, that the things we do should be those which are the will of God (Matthew 3:15).

The Apostle Paul explained to the Philippians about God's work in them, "Therefore, my beloved, as you have always obeyed, not as in my presence only, but now much more in my absence, work out your own salvation with fear and trembling; for it is God who works in you both to will and to do for His good pleasure" (Philippians 2:12-13). It is God creating in His children the desire and the ability to please Him. Even good works are not done out of the arm of the flesh, but by the grace of God.

**ACTION POINT: Let us pray that God will continue to work in us.**

## Spittin' Image

I read in an etymological dictionary years ago that the origination of the colloquial expression "spittin' image" was actually from the phrase, "spirit and image." If you're from the south, you may have heard it said, "That boy is the spittin' image of his father." He is the spirit and image of his dad. His temperament, who he is, and how he looks is the same as his father. As children of God, we, too, should be the spirit and image of our Father.

If it could be said that I am the "spittin' image" of my earthly dad, I would be proud. With regard to him, it was my desire to please him (well... once I matured a bit). I knew that he liked his feet rubbed, his head massaged, good manners, good grades, etc. I knew that honesty and integrity were the cornerstones of his character; hence, they are mine, also. Into my life, I incorporated what was important to my dad. I added things to it— picked up my own flavors of things, but his testimony—his eulogy—I pray will be mine, also.

In the same way, we should desire to be the "spittin' image" of our heavenly Father. His desires should become our desires. His thoughts should be our thoughts. What is important to the Lord should be important to us. Our goal in life should be to please Him with our lives—who we are and what we do.

### Mini-Me

I have one daughter. People say she looks just like me. We don't see it, but others comment on it. She's a mini-me. Our hair is a similar color and our build is similar. Sometimes, I can look at her arm and it's like looking at my own. My husband says that she doesn't just look like me, but she acts like me. We happen to have the same personality type and we have the same thought processes and quirks. In the same way that my daughter is a mini-me, we should resemble the Lord in this manner. Our desire should be for us to be like Him—not by genetics, but by choice. We look like Him and our likes should be what He likes.

### Imitators of Him

Our obedience to the Lord will accomplish His will. God wants us to grow spiritually and produce fruit for His Kingdom, and the Bible tells us how:

> You will have great wisdom and understanding in spiritual things so that you will live the kind of life that HONORS & PLEASES the Lord in EVERY WAY. You will produce fruit in every good work and grow in the knowledge of God" (Colossians 1:9-10, TEV, emphasis added).

This is a wonderful Scripture with a life-changing promise. The Lord makes great wisdom and understanding available to us. It's not just a little wisdom or some wisdom, but GREAT wisdom! Why does He give us that great wisdom and understanding? This verse says the sole reason for us to have that wisdom and understanding is so that our life can honor and please Him in every way. Are we to please God only on Sundays? Are we to please God only when someone else is looking? God gives us what we need to please and honor Him in every thing we do—every thing we say and every thing we think. The end of that verse says that the result of honoring and pleasing the Lord is that we will bear fruit in our pursuits and we will know God. Our relationship with the Father will be a growing fruitful relationship.

One aspect of Jesus being our owner, ruler, and master is that He wants us to look like Him. We are to be molded and shaped into His image.

The Lord wants to live His life through us. He wants us to see through His eyes and touch with His hands, and speak with His words. As we are pliable in the hands of our loving Father, we become more like the Lord Jesus. Will we ever be sinless? No. The Bible says we all sin. Is there a place of perfection on this earth for mankind? No. What we can do, however, is to keep our heart right and repent when we mess up.

God is not looking for perfection, He's looking for love. We must notice that the number one thing all humans have in common is the need to be loved; God is the one who had that desire first. In the plan of salvation, God loved the world enough to allow Jesus to take our sin so that we could take His righteousness. He put us in right standing with God. The Father God sees us through the blood that Jesus shed. The Lord has allowed me to be a partaker of His hope (1 Corinthians 9:10) and His righteousness. My righteousness is as filthy rags, but His is glorious.

Jesus is our example. We are to do the things that He did. The Apostle Paul wrote to the church at Ephesus, "Therefore be imitators of God as dear children. And walk in love, as Christ also has loved us and given Himself for us, an offering and a sacrifice to God for a sweet-smelling aroma" (Ephesians 5:1-2). The Amplified Bible translates this Greek passage with a little more description, "THEREFORE BE imitators of God [copy Him and follow His example], as well beloved children [imitate their father]."

We can be assured that as we imitate Jesus in our daily lives, our lives will be pleasing to the Father God. The Lord honored Jesus and glorified Him because Jesus chose to obey Him and bring delight to His Father. The Apostle Peter records in 2 Peter 1:17-18, "For He received from God the Father honor and glory when such a voice came to Him from the Excellent Glory: 'This is My beloved Son, in whom I am well pleased.'" God couldn't stand it anymore; He had to announce how proud He was of His Son over heaven's loud speaker.

**ACTION POINT: Let us pray that we are molded and shaped into His image.**

# Chapter 7

# Making God Our Delight

## It's All About Him

Scripture is filled with references that we are to make the Lord our delight. We are exhorted to find delight in His presence, in His Word, and in His love. When we find our pleasure in God, He promises us certain benefits.

## Benefits of Making God Our Delight

The first benefit is from the Book of Psalms which says that if we delight ourselves in the Lord, He will give us the desires of our heart (Psalm 37:4). When we mold our will to God's, He places His desires in our heart. Desire is the key to purpose. The process of delight—process of communing with God—reveals desires already placed in your heart. I have heard this verse used as a genie in a bottle, "If we delight in God, He'll give us whatever we want." However, the sincere Christian is not seeking for power or gain, but for the face of God. If you delight in God, He will put the desire in your heart to direct you toward your purpose in life. The first step in living out your purpose can be discovered through interaction with God and confirmed by the Word. God will give you the desires of your heart.

If we keep our heart pure and keep our relationship with Him first and foremost, all the other things will come to us. We may have to occupy our promises—protect and confess—as the children of Israel occupied the Promised Land, but God will give us the victory. As we go about our daily lives, God expects us to keep our priorities in order.

The second benefit of delighting in God is that He will make His way known to us. Job 22:28 says, "Light will shine on your ways ." Our path becomes more sure and our way becomes more obvious. Those are promises for us as we capture the heart of God and make Him our delight.

It is essential for the child of God to make the Lord their delight. You must fall in love with Him and His Word. You must hunger and thirst after His presence. That's all about you! For the most part, the rest of this book you are reading is all about Him. Making God our delight is the key to our survival. The remaining chapters here will focus on our becoming God's delight. We will explore the things He has said will get His attention. We will see what makes the Creator of the Universe incline Himself towards you! My heart's desire—and I trust it is yours—is that I can be trusted to do His will and behave like Jesus in the earth. I want my Heavenly Father to be proud of me. Religion is about rules, regulations, and group ethics. Christianity is not a religion, but a relationship. Being a Christian is all about God and what He's done!

We make the Lord our delight as we seek Him each day. As Moses knew the ways of God, we, too, must learn

His ways. Communion with the Creator should not be on our to-do list so we can check it off. I can only imagine how my husband would feel if I had to check a box to remind me to hug him. It is not drudgery or a law that we seek the Lord daily, but those who delight in God delight in approaching Him.

> Yet they seek me daily, and delight to know my ways, as a nation that did righteousness, and forsook not the ordinance of their God: they ask of me the ordinances of justice; they take delight in approaching to God (Isaiah 58:2, KJV).

**ACTION POINT: Let us pray that we live our lives to put a smile on God's face.**

## Sowing and Reaping

As we talk about this, we must consider one major principle of the Kingdom of God which is sowing and reaping. I've heard this referred to as the Law of Reciprocity which comes from Galatians 6:7. It says, "Do not be deceived, God is not mocked; for whatever a man sows, that he will also reap." The Lord is not messing around here; He's speaking plainly and simply. My interpretation of this is: Don't fool yourself...God refuses to be challenged, ridiculed, or defied. He's not going to be deluded or confused. God's intended purpose is that if you sow or plant something—you're going to reap or harvest the same thing. God does not want us to be confused or deceived about this principle. He makes things clear to us. The farmer sows seed in the field and reaps a predictable harvest. A farmer does not sow tomato seeds and reap beans. If a farmer sows watermelon seeds, he has an expectation that watermelon will multiply in his field. The same is true with the principles of the Kingdom. If you sow kindness, you'll reap kindness – not necessarily from the same person to whom you sowed kindness, but you will reap it. If you sow hatred, your harvest will be hatred. If you give yourself completely to God, God will give Himself completely to you. You will capture His heart by giving Him yours!

As we delight in Him, He will delight in us. The Lord does not expect anything out of us that He does not first offer Himself. As we delight in the Lord, He will find delight in us.

### Delight and Favor

Let us examine one word which is translated as "delight." In the ***Strong's Exhaustive Hebrew Concordance*** it is the verb *chaphets* which originally means: "to bend, hence, to incline, to take pleasure in." The essence of this word is that as we please God, His response will be to bend towards us or be inclined towards us. *Chaphets* is a verb which connotes action. When God finds delight in us, it will bring Him to action on our behalf.

***Webster's Dictionary*** translates "delight" as "to take great pleasure; to satisfy greatly; please." The mission of a Christian should be to satisfy God. Our exhortation from the Apostle Paul is to "walk worthy of the Lord unto all pleasing, being fruitful in every good work, and increasing in the knowledge of God" (Colossians 1:10, KJV). Our goal should not be to satisfy man or self. The Bible exhorts us that we should be "not as pleasing men, but God"

(1 Thessalonians 2:4, KJV). Our goal should be to become a God-pleaser, not a man-pleaser. It should be our desire to live a life that is granted the favor of God first and man second (Proverbs 3:4). However, if the two ever diverge, it should be God's favor that we seek.

## Our Daily Goal

Jesus, our example, was well-pleasing to His Father God. Thayer's defines the Greek word *eudokeoo* as "to be favorably inclined toward one." God says He wants to bestow His favor on me and be inclined towards me. What a promise! What a life goal!

I have thought about what I wanted God to say when I arrive in heaven. My final goal has always been a desire to hear the Lord say: "Well done, good and faithful servant." I want the summation of my life to be that I was good and faithful in the Lord's eyes. That is an excellent futuristic goal for which we live one day at a time. In addition to that statement, today I want to hear God say about me what He said about Jesus. On a daily basis, I want to hear, "This is my beloved child in whom I am well-pleased."

**ACTION POINT: Let us pray that we may be like Jesus and be well-pleasing to the Lord.**

## How Do We Make the Lord Our Delight?

Job 27:10 says, "Will he delight himself in the Almighty? Will he always call on God?" Making God our delight is our choice. Since the Lord's mercy is new every day, we start each day with a clean slate. It would be wisdom to make this choice daily. An indicator of delighting in the Lord is calling on Him at all times. We delight in the Lord by praying to Him and talking to Him. Our communion with Him becomes our very life and our sustaining force.

David never hides his reliance on the Word of God; he tells us that it kept him from perishing in his weaknesses. The Apostle Paul tells us in Romans 7:22 that we delight in God by loving His Word. The Word becomes our counselor to show us the way and guide us into God's truth (Psalm 119:24). As we delight in the Lord, the Lord will delight in us. We see how a Christian should behave and the results of that behavior in Psalm 1:2-3:

> But his delight is in the law of the LORD, And in His law he meditates day and night. He shall be like a tree Planted by the rivers of water, That brings forth its fruit in its season, Whose leaf also shall not wither; And whatever he does shall prosper.

If we delight in God daily, it will make us like a strong and luscious tree unmoved by circumstance and yielding bountiful fruit. Our reward for loving the Lord becomes prosperity in everything we do. Now, that's a promise!

## Our Road Map for Life

The Bible is our road map for life. It is our guide and our light. One of my favorite chapters in the Word is Psalm

119; it's also the longest chapter in the entire Bible. The subtitle for chapter 119 in my Bible is: "Meditations on the Excellencies of the Word of God." God's Word is excellent—extraordinary—superior.

Psalm 119 is about the love we should have for the Word and what it will do in our lives. As we delight in the Word (Psalm 119:77, 143, 174), we are told that it becomes a lamp to our feet and a light to our path (Psalm 119:105). It will shine on our road of life to ensure our steps are steady and straight; the Word will keep you on the right path and make sure you get to your destination in life. In this day and age of insecurity and questions about the future, it is calming to have an anchor for your soul that will guide you to your destiny.

If we don't daily make the Word our delight, we may be destroyed or disappear in our own distress and pain. The burden would be too great (Psalm 119:92). Peter said that the Bible was a more sure word of prophecy—greater than the voice heard from heaven. The Bible is dependable and trustworthy.

**ACTION POINT: Let's choose to build our lives upon the Rock of the Word of God.**

# Chapter 8

# The Righteous Please God

## Commission

God gave us the Great Commission to go into all the world and preach the Good News to everyone. This commission requires us to do something. A commission requires action. There are two things which result in our being formed into the image of Jesus: commissions and omissions. As Christians, we have a commission to do certain things and we have a mandate to omit certain things from our lives. We renew our mind to God's commissions and train ourselves to be disciplined because of our love for and desire to please the Lord. The omissions should be removed from our lives for the same reasons.

## The Upright Walk in Favor

Habakkuk 2:4 says, "The [rigidly] just and the [uncompromisingly] righteous man shall live by his faith and in his faithfulness" (AMP). Faith is the key that unlocks every Christian door. You must have faith in Jesus Christ as the Son of God to be saved from your sin. If you have been saved or born again, you will then live or operate by your faith.

If you live by faith, you have found favor in God's eyes. It is impossible to please God without faith, and it is possible to please God with faith. *Favor* and *delight* are similar in definition. *Delight* means to bend towards. The Hebrew definition of *favor* is *to bend or stoop in kindness*. God's favor or pleasure is for the upright of heart which causes Him to lean towards us and to come to us. In Proverbs it is written, "But among the upright there is favor" (Proverbs 14:9). God is bending toward us in His kindness. The King has stooped down to His subjects to grant their requests. His favor should be our goal and our passion. Why? We were created to bring pleasure to our majestic King. His desires become our desires, and His Kingdom work becomes our Kingdom work as we are molded into His image. His mind becomes our mind as we allow the renewal process to take place through the washing of the water of the Word of God. We are the children of God accomplishing His purposes on the earth and in the heavenlies. In doing these works, our Heavenly Father is pleased.

What do the upright look like? What are their similar characteristics? The upright have made Jesus Christ their Lord and are saved from their sin. The upright are spiritually born-again as new creations to serve their King. The upright are identified in the Bible as those who are:

- Cleansed by the blood of Jesus & innocent from sin (Psalm 19:13)
- Partakers of God's righteousness (Psalm 36:10)
- Praising God (Psalm 33:1)
- Perfect or mature (Psalm 37:37)

- Found in the assembly or church (Psalm 111:1)
- Strengthened by the way of the Lord (Proverbs 10:29)
- Integrity is their guide (Proverbs 11:3)
- Speak deliverance (Proverbs 12:6)
- Depart from evil (Proverbs 16:17)
- Hated by the bloodthirsty (Proverbs 29:10)
- An abomination to the wicked (Proverbs 29:27)

With every command of God, there is a benefit or promise when we obey. When we live an upright life His rewards are extended to us. God's Word reports that there are many benefits for the upright. The list includes that the upright:

- Shall be saved (Psalm 7:10)
- Shall be looked upon by God (Psalm 11:7)
- Shall be protected (Psalm 37:14-15)
- Shall be partakers of an everlasting inheritance (Psalm 37:18)
- Shall be at peace (Psalm 37:37)
- Shall have dominion (Psalm 49:14)
- Shall see God's glory (Psalm 64:10)
- Shall be glad (Psalm 97:11)
- Shall have mighty seed on the earth (Psalm 112:2)
- Shall be blessed (Psalm 112:2)
- Shall be a light in the darkness (Psalm 112:4)
- Shall dwell in God's presence (Psalm 140:13)
- Shall dwell in the land (Proverbs 2:21)
- Shall have a house that flourishes (Proverbs 14:11)
- Shall possess good things (Proverbs 28:10)

The upright or the righteous are those who have been cleansed by the blood of Jesus from their sin.

Becoming upright is by grace and not by works. Anything we do is done only by the grace of God. We have no cause to brag or be prideful about becoming upright. We read in Ephesians 2:8-9, "For by grace you have been saved through faith, and that not of yourselves; it is the gift of God, not of works, lest anyone should boast." Salvation is a free gift to anyone who will believe. It is through faith in the completed work of Jesus Christ so that it might be given to us by the grace or undeserved favor of God. Paul exhorts us to maintain the proper attitude about being a Christian. He says, "But God forbid that I should boast except in the cross of our Lord Jesus Christ" (Galatians 6:14).

**ACTION POINT: Let us choose to be upright before God and man.**

### Right Standing

We have discussed the characteristics of the upright and the benefits of living an upright life. Another thing that succeeds in getting God's attention is righteousness. What is righteousness? Let us delve into this definition from the Hebrew and Greek. It is an Old Testament Hebrew word "tsaddiyq" meaning "just, lawful or righteous." In the New Testament, the Greek word "dictions" is explained as being, "equitable (in character or act); by implication, innocent, holy (absolutely or relatively)." The flesh has no means of becoming justified or being made right; however, through His sacrifice, Jesus has made us righteous unto God. God takes delight in those who receive His Son Jesus into their lives and heart. Jesus was made unto us wisdom, righteousness, sanctification, and redemption (1 Corinthians 1:3). We do not deserve a right-standing with God, but Jesus has given us that position and it pleases the Lord when we receive it.

## Pursuing Righteousness

It is recorded in Proverbs 15:9, "The LORD detests the way of the wicked but he loves those who pursue righteousness" (NIV). The word "pursue" is a verb connoting action which means "to follow in an effort to overtake or capture; chase; to strive to gain or accomplish." It is pleasing to God when we actively pursue a life of right-standing with Him. There is nothing we can do to earn righteousness. There is nothing we can do to be found worthy. However, God loves it when we pursue or chase His character and nature through our relationship with Him.

Along the same thought, King David cried out to the Lord about his own righteousness in Psalm 51. David tells the Lord, "You don't desire a sacrifice and You're not pleased with a burnt offering." He goes on to write, "The sacrifices of God are a broken spirit, A broken and a contrite heart—These, O God, You will not despise... then You shall be pleased with the sacrifices of righteousness," (Psalm 51:17-19). The sacrifice which God looks for is a broken and contrite spirit. If a rancher breaks a horse, he doesn't kill him; the horse doesn't walk around depressed. My grandfather trained horses and when he broke one, he was teaching it to follow his commands. Just like the rancher, God looks for a heart that is submitted to His will and purpose. The Lord is not pleased when we go our own way, but He is pleased when we are fully submitted to Him.

The only sacrifice the Father is interested in is our will submitted to Him. His ultimate goal for us is obedience.

We need to have confidence that He knows best. His ways are not our ways; our ways are not His ways. The importance of hearing the voice of the Lord and obeying it can be found in 1 Samuel 15:22, "So Samuel said: 'Has the LORD as great delight in burnt offerings and sacrifices, As in obeying the voice of the LORD? Behold, to obey is better than sacrifice, And to heed than the fat of rams.'" Even in the day of literal sacrifices and burnt offerings, the Lord made it clear that He took greater joy in His people hearing His voice and doing His will. Our promise is that we do hear the voice of the Good Shepherd and a stranger's voice we will not follow!! How much greater is His desire for obedience today?

The road to self-will and rebellion is wide and leads to destruction, but the road to submission and obedience is narrow and this road leads to life (Matthew 7:13-14). The path to empty yourself and become full of God is not easy, but the joy of becoming like the Lord Jesus will far outweigh the cost. The person on the narrow road will find the favor of the Lord. Our heart's cry should be more of Jesus, less of me.

As we choose to walk as children of the light and exhibit the fruit of the Spirit, in all goodness, righteousness and truth, we find out what is acceptable or pleasing to the Lord. (Ephesians 5:9-10)

**ACTION POINT: Let us pray that our hearts are totally submitted to God.**

## Righteousness – vs – Holiness

Righteousness is a gift—a judgment that says you are in right standing with God through the work accomplished by Jesus Christ. This happens when you become a Christian. It is not based on your efforts and works, but on what Jesus has done. Since God can have no fellowship with sin, we must confess our sin and He is faithful and just to not only forgive us, but to cleanse us, too.

Holiness is a person's personal aspiration to be like the Lord who admonished us by saying, "Be holy, for I am holy" (1 Peter 1:16). God has the expectation for us to live a holy life. However, we can't do it by the arm of the flesh so He gave us the Holy Spirit to help us.

American pastor A.W. Tozer said, "The holy man is not one who cannot sin. A holy man is one who will not sin." The desire of every Christian should be to live right and do right things. "Right" equals "good" as defined by the Bible. We don't live according to the Law adhering to a list of "thou shalt nots." Some look at Christianity as not being able to do wrong things—a long list of stuff you "can't" do. Our attitude should be more of a matter of not wanting to do wrong things. We must train our senses to understand the difference between good and evil. As we renew our minds, we stop wanting to do wrong things.

**ACTION POINT: Choose to walk in personal holiness as you desire to please the Lord. Allow the Holy Spirit to help you pursue this goal.**

# Chapter 9

# How to Please God

## Fellowship with God

The call of God is without repentance. When God issues an assignment, He does not change His mind. Paul expounded more specifically on what the call of God is for Christians. He said, "God is faithful, by whom ye were called unto the fellowship of his Son Jesus Christ our Lord" (1 Corinthians 1:9, KJV). God has called us to fellowship with Him. The Lord desires communion once again with his children. He desires to have sweet fellowship with you just like He had with Adam as they met in the garden in the cool of the day. God wants us to fellowship with Him. There is no harmony, unity or oneness without fellowship. I have a call on my life to fellowship with God and so do you!

There is no confusion as to what "fellowship" means when we are with our friends. Sometimes we can over-spiritualize things in our daily Christian life. The Greek word for "fellowship" is *koinonia* which simply means *to have communion, be a partaker or to partner.* To have communion with the Lord, we are to share a common unity. We have been called to be God's partner and to stay in a common union with Him. He has made us co-laborers in Christ and joint-heirs with Jesus. Our mission is to labor in the vineyard of God's Kingdom and allow the Lord to use us to accomplish His purposes. We are to work towards the common unity of man and God by demonstrating the good works of God to the world.

Communion is talking to the Lord and enjoying His fellowship. During the cool of the day, Adam fellowshipped with God. When he sinned, that privilege was lost—not just for Adam, but the entire human race. When Adam sinned, that sin contaminated the blood line of humanity. However, when we accept Jesus' payment for our sin, we can again enjoy fellowship with the Father.

**ACTION POINT: Let us take advantage of our free gift of restored fellowship which had such a high price.**

As we look at the life of Enoch, we see that he walked with God and pleased Him (Hebrews 11:5). The Amplified Bible summarizes his life, "Enoch walked [in habitual fellowship] with God" (Genesis 5:22, AMP). It pleased God for Enoch to walk with Him and stay in continual fellowship with Him. The heavenly Father desires for His children to spend time with Him. This word *walk* implies a continual walking. It was Enoch's habit to meet with the Lord. Because of their sweet fellowship, Enoch never had to suffer the pangs of death. At the end of three hundred sixty five years, the Heavenly Father received Enoch to Himself in heaven without going through the doorway of death.

God desires our fellowship and He wants us to treasure our time with Him. The Psalmist wrote, "As the deer pants for the water brooks, So pants my soul for You, O God. My soul thirsts for God, for the living God" (Psalm 42:1-2). We must have Him for our survival. As the deer craves water, we are to crave the very heart of God. The book of Hebrews assures the Christian that God will reward those who diligently seek Him (Hebrews 11:6). Those who diligently crave the presence of God will be rewarded by Him.

**ACTION POINT: Let us take time to commune and walk with God daily.**

## Commit to Please God Through Prayer

The Lord's desire for His church is to be called "a house of prayer" (Luke 19:46). The church of God is not a building, but it is composed of individuals all over the world with a common king and a common destiny. Peter writes, "You also, as living stones, are being built up a spiritual house" (1 Peter 2:5). We are God's spiritual house and that house should be "a house of prayer." We are to be a people of prayer. Prayer is defined as to ask, to beseech, to entreat or to call to one's aid. We should continually call upon God for His aid and believe that He will do what He said He would do.

God delights in our prayer. Proverbs 15:8 says, "The prayer of the upright is His delight." He finds great pleasure when His children seek His involvement in their lives and the lives of others. God wants to come to our aid; He is a God that hears and answers our prayers. We are taught that if we ask for bread, our heavenly Father will not give us a stone. If we ask for fish, we won't receive a scorpion. God hears and answers our prayers as we pray according to His Word.

As Christians, we are from Abraham's lineage. Hebrews declares, "He does give aid to the seed of Abraham" (Hebrews 2:16). The Lord tells us over and over in the Scriptures that if we will call, He will answer us. That's a promise upon which we can rely.

There are many types of prayer: intercession, consecration, dedication, faith, and thanksgiving, to name a few. Christians are expected to pray without ceasing or have an attitude of prayerfulness. Regardless of the type of prayer in which we are involved, the Lord expects us to seek His help. All power has been given to Jesus and then He gave it to us. God likes it when we invoke the authority that He's given us. He likes it when we use our faith to take new ground for the Kingdom in the Name of Jesus. He likes it when we whisper our thanks to him or we issue a command to spiritual wickedness in high places. Prayer should be part of every aspect of our lives.

God does not want us to have a roller coaster prayer life. I am not referring to a prayer you pray while riding roller coasters. Roller coaster prayer is the up and down prayer life that so many of God's people experience. There are times when there is continuous prayer and times when there is prayerlessness—feast or famine. We need balance in all things. Sometimes we allow things to distract us from our personal devotional time, our time of interceding for others, or our time of warfare to enforce Jesus' victory in the earth. We must take time to bring our petitions to the One who can solve all of our problems and meet all of our needs. It is essential to make that daily connection with our Lord and King and hear His directives for us each day. He is our life and energy force. In the book of Job, Elihu instructs that if we pray to God, He will find delight in us (Job 33:26). How can we please God? We must have a desire to pray and we must actually do it.

## Worship

Earlier, we saw that God is searching for those who have given Him their whole heart. God also is seeking for true worshipers. Worship is the act of entering into His presence and honoring who He is. The Lord has called us to worship Him—and only Him. When God "seeks" something, He goes on a quest or search. He is looking for His children to worship Him in the spirit and with an honest and sincere heart. John 4:23 says, "But the hour is coming, and now is, when the true worshipers will worship the Father in spirit and truth; for the Father is seeking such to worship Him."

**ACTION POINT: Let's determine to become true worshipers and worship in spirit and truth.**

## A Lesson from Job

> If you return to the Almighty, you will be built up; You will remove iniquity far from your tents. Then you will lay your gold in the dust, And the gold of Ophir among the stones of the brooks. Yes, the Almighty will be your gold And your precious silver; For then you will have your delight in the Almighty, And lift up your face to God. You will make your prayer

> to Him, He will hear you, And you will pay your vows. You will also declare a thing, And it will be established for you; So light will shine on your ways. When they cast you down, and you say, 'Exaltation will come!' Then He will save the humble person. He will even deliver one who is not innocent; Yes, he will be delivered by the purity of your hands (Job 22:23-30).

There is much controversy over the truth found in the oldest book of the Bible. We are not going to examine the text in whole, but we are going to look at Eliphaz's words to Job. In this passage, a picture of what it looks like to please God is painted. When you delight in the Lord, you will:

- lift up your face to God (v. 26)
- pray to Him (v. 27)
- pay your vows (v. 27)
- decree a thing (v. 28)

The result from this lifestyle is that God will answer your prayers; He will establish the things that you speak forth which agree with His Word, and finally we have the guarantee that light will shine on our ways. We need the Lord to shine on our ways; His light will allow us to walk in the path He has chosen for us.

## Chapter 10

# Two Essentials in Pleasing God

### Salvation Gets You into the Family

The most critical thing for any individual person is to learn about and receive God's grace through the completed work of Jesus Christ. Once we are Christians, the Lord sets forth a standard in which we are to walk. These things are not what will get you into heaven or keep you out, but they are right and good things to make you more like your Father God. Just as parents love their children because they are family, the parents still have a code of conduct to pass on and a standard of behavior to enforce in their children. Parents find pleasure in children who follow their guidance for life. God is the same way.

### Two Essentials

In the Scriptures, we see there are two essential things that must be found in the life of a Christian who wants to please God. There are a many things which please Him, but two are essential. Without these two things, you can't please God—it's plain and simple. As Christians, we must walk in faith and walk in the spirit.

If you want to become God's delight, you must first have faith because without it, it is impossible to please Him. There is no way around it. You cannot please God without faith.

Secondly, you must walk in the spirit. We exist as a spirit, but we live in a body. Our fleshly earth suits are full of fleshly desires and needs that are oftentimes contrary to God's desires. When we walk in the spirit, we allow the Holy Spirit to live and flow through us. Through God's Spirit, the fullness of God can be expressed in us to the world.

### #1—Faith

Christianity is built upon faith in God. The Bible describes faith as the substance of things hoped for and the evidence of things you cannot see (Hebrews 11:1). We must have faith to enter God's Kingdom and we must maintain faith to live in it. We press on toward the prize of the high calling in Christ Jesus by faith. Faith comes from hearing the Word of God and it is expressed through our obedience to that Word. It is absolutely impossible to please God without faith. Hebrews 11:6 says:

> But without faith it is impossible to please and be satisfactory to Him. For whoever would come near to God must [necessarily] believe that God exists and that He is the rewarder of those who earnestly and diligently seek Him [out] (AMP).

How do we please God? We please Him by our faith. Faith is our title deed in the unseen, spiritual world. As we receive things in the spiritual realm, the answer will show up in the physical world. In the beginning, God spoke and there was light. He has placed that power in us as we agree with His Word. Life and death are contained in the words we speak (Proverbs 18:21). This pleases God when we speak commands of faith for His purposes.

## Growing Faith

To every man is given the measure of faith (Romans 12:3) for salvation, but it is up to us to allow our faith to grow continually. Faith is dynamic and is always increasing or decreasing depending on what you are doing. How do we allow our faith to grow? Faith **comes** by hearing the Word of God. We can try to complicate this and grunt, strain, and fast meals, but God is simple: faith **comes**. As we continue to hear His Word, we increase in faith. The Apostle Paul writes in 2 Thessalonians 1:3, "We are bound to thank God always for you, brethren, as it is fitting, because your faith grows exceedingly." Paul was thankful that their faith was growing. God is glorified when our faith is growing.

In the beginning of our walk with God, our faith is compared to the size of a tiny mustard seed (Mark 4:31). However, when it is full grown, it becomes a large tree which provides shelter to the birds. The same is true with our faith. It starts out small—just the measure that God gave you when you were first born-again—but, when you hear the Word, your faith will grow and impact the lives of the people around you.

## Expressions of Faith

We can express our growing faith in several ways. The main way to express a faith that pleases God is through our obedience. Obedience is a commitment to obey God's

Word, not to just hear it. Hearing the Word and doing it makes us like the man who built his house on the solid rock. When the winds and waves came, his house stood. The other guy heard the same Word and did not choose to practice it and His house was washed away. Jesus Christ is the Solid Rock upon which we build our house and our obedience to His Word will keep our house strong.

We must live by faith, and we must stay the course. The book of Hebrews says, "And those whose faith has made them good in God's sight must live by faith, trusting him in everything. Otherwise, if they shrink back, God will have no pleasure in them" (Hebrews 10:38, TLB). God takes pleasure when we press on towards our high calling in Jesus Christ full of faith and power while obeying the Word of truth. He is displeased when we pause to doubt Him. Like Lot's wife, when we have second thoughts, we come out from under God's divine protection. Without faith, it is impossible to please God.

Faith is the gift of God through which we may be saved. Then, as we work with the measure of faith we have been given, our faith will grow and God will have more opportunities to move in our lives. In Acts 6:8, we wee that Stephen was full of faith. Let us commit to be like Stephen and be full of faith and power and we will allow God to do great signs and wonders through us.

**ACTION POINT: Daily choose to do things to make your faith grow.**

### #2—Walk in the Spirit

The Apostle Paul writes in Romans 8:8, "So then, those who are in the flesh cannot please God" (NKJV). This does not mean that if you have flesh and bones that you cannot please the Lord. However, it is speaking in terms of those who walk after the flesh; those who seek to fulfill the desires of the flesh will not capture the Lord's heart. It is impossible to please God if you walk in the flesh. God is pleased by those who choose to walk in the spirit and not allow the flesh to consume them (Galatians 5:16). Part of our Christian inheritance is the ability to walk in the spirit beyond the limits and desires of our humanity. One of our free gifts from God is that we have His Spirit in us to help us follow Him. The Holy Spirit is an ever-present help in time of need; He's got our back. God is pleased when we walk in the supernatural – not limited to the natural. The natural human mind and flesh are at war with the re-created and renewed Christian spirit. The Bible explains it this way:

> Because the carnal mind is enmity against God...So then, those who are in the flesh cannot please God. But you are not in the flesh but in the Spirit, if indeed the Spirit of God dwells in you (Romans 8:7-9).

It becomes clear what pleases God when we see what does not please Him. Walking in the flesh does not please the Lord, and He does not receive glory when we allow the works of the flesh to rule us.

## Identity Theft

What establishes your identity? With what do you identify? Some parents are more interested in the profession their child pursues than who their child becomes—their character—their personhood. God is not that way; He cares more about who we are—not what we are. It's not always so important if your child is a professor, artist, dancer, mathematician, or chemist, because those things can change in an instant; in and of themselves, they don't have eternal value. However, the person that your child becomes is an eternal journey and no one can take it from you.

We can get so involved in our careers... or our ministries. We're going places; we're on the way up. Even the best of intentions may declare, "Lord, let me do something for you." Our destiny is important, but the journey gives us our true identity. The wise journeyer will ensure that they are prepared for their destiny—or destination. One definition of success is when preparation meets opportunity. As we go about our daily lives, success comes as we are molded and shaped into His image. As we go, we become more in synch with His Spirit. As we go, we become more of the spirit and image of our Father. On the road to my destiny, I become.

Do you remember when Samuel was a boy and heard someone calling his name? Samuel was a young boy and he thought Eli called to him. However, Eli was a man learned in the ways of the Lord—a man of spiritual understanding and authority and it still took three times for him to realize the Lord called to Samuel. Jesus said that His people hear His voice and they don't follow strangers. God's speaking. Is anybody listening?

**ACTION POINT: Stay true to your identity in Christ.**

### Lust of the Flesh

The lust of the flesh is a worldly craving or desire for things that please our natural human appetites. "For all that is in the world—the lust of the flesh, the lust of the eyes, and the pride of life—is not of the Father but is of the world" (1 John 2:16). We cannot capture the heart of God by walking in the flesh. What are the lusts of the flesh? There is a list in Galatians 5:19-21:

> Now the doings (practices) of the flesh are clear (obvious): they are immorality, impurity, indecency, idolatry, sorcery, enmity, strife, jealousy, anger (ill temper), selfishness, divisions (dissensions), party spirit (factions, sects with peculiar opinions, heresies), envy, drunkenness, carousing, and the like. I warn you beforehand, just as I did previously, that those who do such things shall not inherit the kingdom of God (AMP).

What's a person to do? We have these natural desires which conflict with God's best for us. Do we just wrestle with our flesh until we go to heaven? No. God has provided a way for us to walk free of these things. Have you ever been on a diet to lose weight? All you could think about is what you were not supposed to eat. The more you thought about NOT eating, the more you wanted to eat. That's the way it is with most things. The best way to stop a bad habit is to replace it with a good one. If you have a bad thought, focus on creating a good thought. Scripture tells us to think on things which are good, pure, honest, and worthy of praise. Replace the works of the flesh with the fruit of the spirit.

## Fruit of the Spirit

We combat the works of the flesh by walking in the spirit. Galatians 5:16 tells us, "Walk in the Spirit, and you shall not fulfill the lust of the flesh." These are the things which combat the fleshly nature: love, joy, peace, longsuffering, kindness, goodness, faithfulness, gentleness, and self-control. (Galatians 5:22-23) Every night when I pray for my daughter, I thank the Lord for the fruit of the spirit in her life. I thank Him in advance—even when I may not consistently see them all in residence. We should pray for the fruit of the spirit to be developed in us as we make a conscious decision to forbid our flesh to have dominion or rule over our lives.

## Overcoming

How do we avoid the appetites of our human nature? First, as we walk after the spirit, we shall live. We are exhorted to "put on the Lord Jesus" (Romans 13:14) to avoid the lusts of the flesh. Paul asks us this question, "Are you so foolish? Having begun in the Spirit, are you now being made perfect by the flesh?" (Galatians 3:3). The answer is a resounding NO! Secondly, we renew our minds to God's Word. We are to let the mind of Christ dwell or reside in us. When we learn what God says about things, we should change our desires to match His desires. The Lord knows our heart. Only He can separate the thoughts and the intentions of our heart. Thirdly, we pray in the Spirit. The book of Jude says that praying in the Holy Ghost will help us avoid walking in ungodly lusts. The race that we run—our Christian life—must begin in the spirit and end in the spirit. Our perfection or maturity does not come through our flesh, but by the Holy Spirit—the Helper—who lives on the inside of every Christian.

**ACTION POINT: Choose to walk in the spirit so you will not fulfill the lusts of the flesh.**

## Chapter 11

# Actions and Attitudes

### Actions

As we stated earlier, it is God's desire that we are imitators of Jesus. Our goal should be to do the things which please the Father. We must always keep in our minds and hearts that salvation is by grace; it cannot be earned. As we keep this attitude, we will always retain a thankful heart to the Lord. However, once we are in the family of God and we become conscious of pleasing Him, we have family responsibilities that we should be doing. There are many things listed in the Bible in which God delights, below are a few:

- the prayer of the righteous (Proverbs 15:8)
- the unity of believers (Psalm 133:1)
- building the house of God (Haggai 1:8-9)
- honesty and fairness (Proverbs 11:1)
- those who deal faithfully (Proverbs 12:22)
- prosperity of His people (Psalm 35:27 and Deuteronomy 30:9)
- finding a wife (Proverbs 18:22)

## Unity

We have already looked at the prayer of the righteous. Let us look at bringing delight to God through our unity. *Unity* is coming together in one mind and one spirit or to be in agreement. First, we must be in unity with our Lord. The prophet Amos asks, "Can two walk together, unless they are agreed?" (Amos 3:3). In order to walk with God, we must be in agreement or in oneness with who He is and what He says. Unity or oneness in the faith is an indicator that we are walking in maturity (Ephesians 4:13).

Another flavor to the word "unity" is *assemblage*. God says that it is pleasant to Him when the saints gather together in a holy assembly. That truth would explain why the Lord later commands that we do not forsake the gathering or assembling with fellow Christians. As Christian churches around the world drop their mid-week or Sunday evening services, God is saying we are to gather more often—not less—and encourage one another more—not less—during these last days.

In addition to assembling together, God is also pleased when we build His house. Our first priority should be to the spiritual house of God which is formed when two or more gather in His name. This can be in your home or at work or wherever two come together in the name of the Lord. The second priority needs to be the physical house of God which is the building that we call holy and set aside to glorify God. This is where Christians gather to teach spiritual truths and encourage each other.

The prophet Haggai declared the word of the Lord, "'Build the temple, that I may take pleasure in it and be glorified,' says the LORD" (Haggai 1:8). God looks on the heart of believers, but He also is honored by the buildings that we set apart for His work.

The Book of Proverbs shares the wisdom of Solomon for daily living. Solomon talks about being honest and fair in every area of our lives. We bring delight to the Lord when we walk in truth and honesty. Proverbs 11:1 reads, "Dishonest scales are an abomination to the LORD, But a just weight is His delight." Dealing honestly in our business, friends, and family brings pleasure to God. The children of God must demonstrate His nature on the earth.

We are a "living epistle" or letter detailing to others about the goodness of God. Hopefully, the world will come to Him because of our good works. We are admonished to find out what's acceptable and pleasing to the Lord so that others may glorify God.

> For you were once in darkness, but now you are light in the Lord. Walk as children of light (for the fruit of the Spirit is in all goodness, righteousness, and truth), finding out what is acceptable to the Lord (Ephesians 5:8-11).

## Attitudes of the Heart

In addition to the things we do, we are to purpose to have certain heart attitudes to obtain God's delight or favor. God delights in those who revere and worship Him and find their hope in His mercy. Psalm 147:11 says, "The LORD takes pleasure in those who fear Him, in those who hope in His mercy." If you ever have a question about whether you have a right attitude, go to the Word. The writer of Hebrews informs us, "For the word of God is living and active... It judges the thoughts and attitudes of the heart" (Hebrews 4:12-13, NIV). Our most honest intentions are laid bare when compared to the Word of God.

## Prosperity

Another thing the Lord delights in is the prosperity of His people. Psalm 35:27 says, "Let them shout for joy and be glad, Who favor my righteous cause; And let them say continually, 'Let the LORD be magnified, Who has pleasure in the prosperity of His servant.'" The word for prosperity here is "shalom" which means the health, prosperity, and peace. The Apostle John told us that his desire and prayer was for all of us to prosper in our business affairs as we prosper in our spiritual lives (3 John 2). Prosperity is not a bad word to God and it should not be to His children.

Look in Deuteronomy at the covenant blessings which God extended to His people. There are blessings for serving God. It doesn't cost to serve God, it pays! The New Covenant interpretation of this blessing is that as we make Jesus our Lord and seek to please God, we will be blessed. The Word says, "The LORD will again delight in you and make you prosperous... if you obey the LORD your God and keep his commands... and turn to the LORD your God with all your heart and with all your soul" (Deuteronomy 30:9-10, NIV). When God is pleased with you and you mix faith with His promises, He will pour out His blessings on you to prosper you.

**ACTION POINT: Prosperity will follow as you choose to come to God with all of your heart and soul.**

## Wives

God said it is not good for man to be alone. Whether we find a mate for life or we look to our family and friends, we were not designed to be by ourselves. Putting prisoners in solitary confinement is considered by some to be psychological torture; the effects of being by yourself manifest in the physical body and in the mind. Marriage is a union set up by God to keep man from being alone. If you're a man and you find a wife, God says you have found a good thing. Period. The wives of the world can take heart that God considers them as "good" as indicated when He said, "He who finds a wife finds a good thing, And obtains favor from the LORD" (Proverbs 18:22). God gives husbands a special favor... I guess they need it.

## Giving Pleases God

> Let each one [give] as he has made up his own mind and purposed in his heart, not reluctantly or sorrowfully or under compulsion, for God loves (He takes pleasure in, prizes above other things, and is unwilling to abandon or to do without) a cheerful (joyous, "prompt to do it") giver [whose heart is in his giving] (2 Corinthians 9:7, AMP).

One money principle in the Bible is that your treasure follows your heart, and your heart follows your treasure. In the Word, the Lord has made it clear that He expects Christians to give tithes and offerings. We'll save a discourse on tithing for another time, but no one can deny that the Kingdom of God is expected to be financed through the faithful giving of its citizens; the Lord expects everyone to participate at some level just like the widow and giving her mite. Some may use guilt to persuade a congregation to give; others use manipulation more designed at getting an emotional response. After we tithe, God instructs us to make up our own minds and purpose in our hearts what to give. Our actions are not to be compelled by external forces. The Lord says that He takes pleasure in cheerful giving done without delay. Let's not begrudge the gifts we present to the Lord. Giving is a natural outgrowth when God has our whole heart. Freely we receive, freely we give.

**ACTION POINT: Remember that as we give to God, He promises to give to us. Whatever a man sows, he will reap. Decide to be a giver today.**

# Chapter 12

# Bible Examples

## The World

When Jesus walked the earth, He consistently referred to Himself as the "Son of man." This phrase refers to the Lord eighty-eight times in the New Testament. Some historians say that this was Jesus' favorite name for Himself. In the beginning, Jesus reigned as the Son of God, but He willingly became the Son of Man. God says, "My delight was with the sons of man" (Proverbs 8:31). Through His resurrection, we have the great exchange. Jesus allows the sons of men who call upon His Name to become the sons of God. God so loved the world that He gave His Son as a sacrifice to allow us to become His sons and daughters.

## The Saints

God finds delight in us when we come into His family. Because of His love, the Lord gave a sacrifice for the entire world to become His children and to become the saints of God. Psalm 16:3 reads, "As for the saints who are in the earth, they are the majestic ones in whom is all my delight" (NAS). All of God's delight or pleasure is found in His children.

In the beginning, the Spirit of the Lord hovered over the face of the earth when it was void and without form. God spoke the worlds into existence. He created man in His image and placed him in a garden east of Eden or the garden of delight. God was a Father who wanted a family.

God has had trying times with His family. Through it all, His love has stayed strong. Even when the Lord wanted to destroy the whole earth and regretted creating man, Noah still found favor in His sight and thereby saved all of mankind. The book of Psalms says, "For the Lord takes pleasure in His people" (Psalm 149:14).

Jesus, the only begotten of the Father, became the first born of many brethren when He sacrificed Himself for all.

Most scholars agree that another name for the church of God is spiritual Zion. The prophet Isaiah speaks into the future that there will be a people who will no longer be called "Forsaken" or "Desolate," but their new name will be *Hephzibah* which means, "My delight is in her." When man was in the Garden of Eden, he was God's delight. After the fall, man became full of sin through the blood line. The prophecy spoke of Zion's new name was telling of the time following the completed work of Jesus Christ when the family of God would once again become the delight of the Father.

## Hall of Faith

Those saints which have gone before us are our examples. We are to learn from what they did and did not do. Their attitudes, thoughts, and actions illustrate those things which are pleasing to God or not pleasing to God.

Abraham was counted as righteous by God because he believed what the Lord told him. He was a real man with real challenges in life. Abraham did not do everything perfectly; however, the testimony at the end of his life was that he was a friend of God. "And the Scripture was fulfilled which says, 'Abraham believed God, and it was accounted to him for righteousness.' And he was called the friend of God" (James 2:23). Abraham brought delight to His Father God.

Another patriarch that brought pleasure to the Lord which we mentioned earlier was Enoch. Enoch walked with the Lord and Hebrews 11:5 says, "…he had this testimony, that he pleased God." We do not know a lot about Enoch, but we are told in several Scriptures that he walked with the Lord. God is pleased when we walk with Him. The more we walk with Him, the more we become like Him. His desires become our desires and His dislikes become our dislikes. It is during these seasons that we come into oneness or unity with the God of the Universe.

Samuel is another example we can follow in pleasing God. Hannah sought the Lord for a child. Her baby grew up to become the prophet Samuel who was dedicated to the Lord before his inception, and he grew up living at the temple in Eli's care. His testimony as a child is recorded, "And the child Samuel grew in stature, and in favor both with the Lord and men" (1 Samuel 2:26). God's favor or delight should be our goal, but the favor of man is important to the Lord, too. I used to say that man's opinion of me didn't matter until I read this verse. It is important to have a good testimony in your community.

The next example of pleasing God is King David who was anything but perfect. The Bible records his various failures. There are consequences for our sin that must play out, but God's forgiveness and acceptance comes when a repentant heart turns away from sin. David was not just sorry for his sin, but he vowed with the Lord's help to turn away from it. The testimony of David was that he found favor with God and was the apple of His eye. David was the very center or pupil of God's eye. David found the favor of God because of His repentant and worshipful heart. The Word says in Acts 13:22-23, "I have found David the son of Jesse, a man after My own heart, who will do all My will." It is a valid goal to desire to turn your heart wholly over to the Lord where you only want those things that God wants. Our testimony should be that we are after God's heart.

Mary, the mother of Jesus found God's pleasure. As a young girl when the angel told her of God's plan to bring the Son of God into the earth, she did not understand and could not comprehend it. The angel told her, "You have found favor with God" (Luke 1:30). The angel then revealed God's plan to use Mary to deliver His Son into the earth. It is necessary for the shepherd to enter through the sheepfold by the door (John 10); the lawful Shepherd of God's people had to be born into the earth. The favor of God on her life allowed the plan of God to be fulfilled in the earth. This favor did not just benefit her life, but it benefited all of humanity.

We may never know the full affects of our actions and choices on those around us.

When we are conformed to the Lord's thoughts and transformed by His Spirit, we become usable in His hands. He can trust us to do His work and accomplish His purposes. Mary's faith-filled response was, "Let it be to me according to your word" (Luke 1:38). She didn't understand it, but she trusted the Lord. We must let God be God and have His way whether we understand it or not. God's favor and delight on our lives qualifies us for greater service.

**ACTION POINT: Choose to be a godly example for the world to see.**

### Jesus, the Christ

The testimony of Jesus is our greatest example. Both Matthew and Peter were eyewitnesses and they recorded Jesus' testimony which was that He was God's beloved Son. Peter recounted their story in 2 Peter 1:17 when God said, "This is My beloved Son in Whom I am well pleased and delight" (AMP).

It was the goal of Jesus to do the Father's work. The Apostle Paul also records, "Christ pleased not Himself" (Romans 15:3). Jesus went about teaching, preaching, and healing. Doing these things brought God's favor to Jesus. Luke writes that Jesus, like Samuel, continued to increase in wisdom, stature, and favor with God and man. Again, it is essential to live life to please God and as we do, the favor of man will be a by-product and will bring glory to God.

Jesus' life is our example of perfection as the Son of God. We are exhorted to be molded and shaped into His image—to be His spirit and image in the earth. We are instructed in Ephesians 5:1, "Therefore be imitators of God [copy Him and follow His example], as well-beloved children [imitate their father]" (AMP). The most important thing a Christian can do is to set their heart to be like their Father God. We need to purpose to do what Jesus did and say what Jesus said. A few years ago, a trendy Christian acronym was popular. People wore bracelets and t-shirts bearing the letters, "WWJD?" What would Jesus do? This is a great thing to ask before we go about life's tasks. Let's make a decision to do what Jesus would do!

**ACTION POINT: Make a decision to live your life as Jesus lived His.**

# Chapter 13

# Displeasing God

## Accentuate the Positive

In the Bible, God has made it very clear what pleases Him and what displeases Him. In order to better understand the things that please Him, we will look more closely at the things that do not.

God loved the children of Israel, but He had issues with their disobedience and their complaining. 1 Corinthians 10:5 shares, "But with most of them God was not well pleased." The result of not pleasing God was that they died in the wilderness and were unable to enter the Promised Land. We can use the experience of the children of Israel as an example of what not to do: don't disobey and don't complain. This is a great life lesson for every area of our lives. Some of us tell our kids not to complain, but we go to our jobs or churches and complain even more ourselves. Brethren, these things ought not to be so.

I normally like to focus on the positive, but I believe in this case that we can greatly learn about the Lord by seeing what He doesn't like. If you're like me, you want to examine each of these items and ensure that they're not part of your life. The list below contains things that are not pleasing to the Lord:

- Divorce (Malachi 2:16) – I think anyone who has been through a divorce would say they didn't like it either. Once you've been joined together, it's incredibly painful to be separated. There are two scriptural reasons for divorce that the Lord excuses: adultery and abandonment. Divorce is not the unpardonable sin as some denominations may claim; there is forgiveness after divorce. However, the bottom line is that the Lord still hates divorce.
- Lust (2 Chronicles 22, Jeremiah 46 & Ephesians 2) – Lust is a consuming desire for something. This sin is not limited to an ungodly sexual desire, but certainly does include it.
- Idolaters – God expects us to worship Him alone; He will not share you with anyone or anything. Is your job an idol? Is your boyfriend an idol? Sometimes a little surgery is required to remove things from our lives. It hurts at first, but we're better off in the end.
- Sexual immorality – This can range from perversions, including pornography to sexting and solicitations. Sexual harassment would also fall into this category.
- Murmuring – This includes complaining and whining like the children of Israel did. Parents don't like for their kids to murmur and complain, and God doesn't like it either.
- Dishonesty (Proverbs 11:1) – Be honest and truthful.

- Lying lips (Proverbs 12:22) – Obvious disregard for the truth.
- Sacrifice of the wicked (Proverbs 15:8) – An offering to God made by someone who does not know Him is not received by Him.
- The way of the wicked (Proverbs 15:9) – Following after wickedness and doing evil; not following after God.
- Death (Ezekiel 18:32) – God values His saints and takes no pleasure when someone dies.
- Fools (Ecclesiastes 5:4) – Those who say there is no God.

## Follow After Wisdom

The Holy Spirit has been given to us to help us serve the Lord and to overcome our weaknesses through God's power. The wisdom of the ages is opened up to the Christian through Jesus since He has been made wisdom to us. God takes no pleasure in fools so the entire book of Proverbs attacks the fool and promotes wisdom. We see that Isaiah, the prophet, writes, "For it is a people of no understanding… He who formed them will show them no favor" (Isaiah 27:11-12).

Since we want to please God, we must become wise. The beginning of wisdom is the fear or reverence of God. Through salvation, we obtain God's righteousness or right standing; through wisdom, we can learn how to apply our knowledge of God and His Word in our daily lives.

**ACTION POINT: Wisdom cries in the street and is available to all through Jesus Christ. Choose to walk in God's wisdom.**

## Avoid Wickedness

David writes, "For You are not a God who takes pleasure in wickedness" (Psalm 5:4). To please God, we must walk in the righteousness Jesus gives us and avoid wickedness. Our salvation does not hinge on our good works and holy living, but we do have a family responsibility to walk uprightly and proudly represent our heavenly Father.

## Displeasure in Death

The next point we will cover is also about God's displeasure. At the same time, I want to offer food for thought. In some church circles, we hear about how God "took" our good brother or sweet sister on to heaven to be with Him. We first see in the Bible, "Precious in the sight of the LORD is the death of his saints" (Psalm 116:15, KJV). The Father God sees the death of His saints as costly and valuable. However, the prophet Ezekiel records God's thought: "I have no pleasure in the death of one who dies" (Ezekiel 18:32, NKJV). The word "death" here means literal death or to die. God does not "take" or kill people. It is the thief that comes to steal, kill and destroy; God comes to bring life (John 10:10). The next time you hear of a saint going to be with the Lord, let's choose our words more carefully. God cares about their passing and counts it as precious and costly, but he takes no pleasure when one dies. It seems like sometimes God gets a bad rap for the devil's work.

## Results of Displeasing God

When I was a child, I always wanted to know the consequences of my possible disobedience. I was a pretty good kid and usually tried to do what was right, but I did appreciate knowing what consequence my good decisions caused me to avoid. As God's children, we too, have consequences for our sin, in addition to it displeasing Him.

In Genesis, sin prevailed in the earth. It grieved God that He had made man and the earth was destroyed. Man's sin caused God's displeasure and He wished He had never created him. Wow! That is serious stuff!

We see that the children of Israel died in the wilderness because God was displeased with their behavior. The Israelites disobeyed and murmured against the Lord, and He was displeased with the majority of the them. The consequence of their actions was that they were to be scattered in the wilderness. 1 Corinthians 10:5 says, "But with most of them God was not well pleased, for their bodies were scattered in the wilderness." God expanded their journey to forty years and then the children of Israel ended up dying before they could reach the promised land.

God's anger was directed towards the Israelites. "Now with whom was He angry forty years? Was it not with those who sinned, whose corpses fell in the wilderness?" (Hebrews 3:17). God's anger will burn towards those who displease Him. Heaven can still be your home, but God can be angry at you.

We have established that it is wise to set our hearts to please God and bring delight to Him. There are great benefits that come when you please Him and there are unpleasant things that come from displeasing Him. These are some of the results of displeasing God:

- Death in the wilderness (1 Corinthians 10:5)
- God's anger (Exodus 4:14)
- Cast out to another land (Jeremiah 16:12-13)

## Balaam

Balaam was another person who aroused God's anger. Balaam's eventual response showed that he knew that God's displeasure was causing His anger to be displayed. The Bible says in Numbers 22:22, "Then God's anger was aroused because he went, and the Angel of the LORD took His stand in the way as an adversary against him." Balaam was not on God's side; he had enemies in high places. Following the incident with the angel of the Lord, Balaam repented and only spoke God's Word thereafter.

## Hated by God

Sunday school classes all over the world learn about God's love and memorize John 3:16. We often hear about His love, but we don't often hear about His hatred. There are some things that God just hates and will not endure.

> There are six things the LORD hates, seven that are detestable to him: haughty eyes, a lying tongue, hands that shed innocent blood, a heart that devises wicked schemes, feet that are quick to rush into evil, a false witness who pours out lies and a man who stirs up dissension among brothers (Proverbs 6:16-19, NIV).

When I first read this verse years ago, I determined in my heart not to be party to any of these offenses. I certainly did not want to be detestable, odious, or vile to the Lord.

Here is a more detailed look at these things which God hates. He hates the snobbish and arrogant; He loves the humble. Lying is a vile sin to God; He loves truthfulness and honesty. The Word of God is truth and the author of it loves truth.

There is forgiveness for murder and abortion, but God still hates it. God protects the innocent. Judas Iscariot is the foremost example of one who shed innocent blood. Before he hanged himself, Judas bemoaned, “I have sinned by betraying innocent blood” (Matthew 27:4).

The Lord hates those who scam people. You can read about these people everyday in the newspaper. Con men and women lie in wait to take from others by trickery—their money, their reputation, their influence, their families. God loves the generous. The Lord doesn’t like it when a person is continually drawn to wickedness. You may hear about a fight going on in a restaurant and everyone runs to watch. I heard on the news not long ago where a young girl was attacked by a gang and hundreds stood around and watched and even videotaped it for the internet. This type of behavior is despicable to the Lord and it should be to us, also.

The last two things which God hates are a false witness and one who stirs up strife. Some people feel so bad about themselves that in order to feel better about themselves, they lie about others. I know of a church person who decided to tell atrocious lies about their pastor. He chose his victims carefully and only lied to new converts. With deceitful words, some try to assassinate another's character. The Bible says, "A good name is to be chosen rather than great riches, loving favor rather than silver and gold" (Proverbs 22:1). The Lord takes it seriously when we try to tear someone down with lies. Thankfully, the truth will usually bubble to the surface, and God will avenge His own family. Finally, the last thing that God hates is a person who purposes to divide and conquer. That person desires to set people at odds and thereby better their own position. Unfortunately, division is a main strategy of the enemy and it's used against families, countries, and even God's own house. An ugly spirit drives these people and they operate under their father, the devil.

God hates these seven things with a great amount of fury and we should, too. These things and the other things mentioned should be on your "absolutely never do" list.

**ACTION POINT: Purpose to be a person of character conviction. Do right things because they are right!**

# Chapter 14

# Results of Pleasing God

## The Goal Is the Prize

The best result you could have when you set your sights on pleasing God is to actually accomplish it. Pleasing the Lord is a reward in and of itself. The best thing you could hear is that God is well-pleased with you. One thing about the Lord, He always works in a win-win mode; you win and He wins. He works for the common good in all things. There is usually a blessing for us which comes with God's favor. The Bible discusses several things which happen when you become the delight of the Father.

## Wisdom, Knowledge, Happiness & Wealth

God promises to give wisdom, knowledge, happiness, and wealth to the person who captures His heart. This might be too much for the religious-minded, but this verse in Ecclesiastes 2:26 says it far better than I could.

> To the man who pleases him, God gives wisdom, knowledge and happiness, but to the sinner He gives the task of gathering and

> storing up wealth to hand it over to the one who pleases God... (NIV).

The Lord takes pleasure in blessing His saints. Just as an earthly father enjoys rewarding his children for making him proud, the Lord does the same. That fact is hard for some to believe. He is a wonderful, loving heavenly Father.

God allowed Solomon to ask for anything, and he asked for wisdom. God was thrilled with his choice. Wisdom is the principle thing – the first thing. A New Testament promise for Christians is that Jesus has been made wisdom to us. The God of all knowledge wants to give that knowledge to us and the wisdom to use it.

The Apostle Paul prayed that we be enriched in all knowledge (1 Corinthians 1:5). Happiness and blessing seem to go hand-in-hand. Joy is a fruit of the spirit, but happiness is based on happenings and the Lord wants us to have happiness in this life. If we humble ourselves to the Lord—like King David did, we will inherit the land (Psalm 37:11) and we "will delight... in ABUNDANT PROSPERITY." The good of the land will be ours.

As I said, pleasing God is worthy of being our life's goal; however, God has promised all of these other blessings to the ones who please Him. He wants to give His kingdom to the ones who have captured His heart.

## The Kingdom

Luke 12:32 says, "It is your Father's good pleasure to give you the kingdom." This word "pleasure" comes from the Greek word *eudokeo* which means "to think well of, i.e. approve (an act); specifically, to approbate (a person or thing)." The Lord thinks well of giving us the kingdom; He approves of the idea. You could also say that He thinks well of us, so He gives us the kingdom.

What is the kingdom of God? The kingdom of God or the kingdom of Heaven is the world of God – His realm of dominion. Entering into the kingdom of God is more than rule keeping; it is obtained by having a personal relationship with the Lord Jesus. There are many Scriptures which talk about the kingdom. It's not just about keeping the Law, because if you live by the Law, you'll be judged by it. That will never come out good for any of us. However, if we live through our forgiveness in Jesus Christ, we'll live by His grace and freedom. I would venture to say that there is a difference in being part of the Kingdom which comes when you believe on Jesus Christ and being given the Kingdom.

## Child of God

Every person on this earth—sinner or saint—has a destiny. Some of us connect up with that destiny and live a fulfilled life. Others don't. It is God's will that we should all partake of the saving grace of Jesus Christ. The course was laid for this destiny by God's good pleasure. Ephesians 1:5 says, "having predestined us to adoption as sons by Jesus Christ to Himself, according to the good pleasure of His will." Our status to receive sonship through Christ Jesus came as a result of it being God's pleasure—His good pleasure. God wanted a family. What a privilege to be part of His family!! His desire is that none are lost. We all have that opportunity.

## Peace

Another promise of pleasing God is found in Proverbs 16:7. We see that for those who capture God's heart, He will, in turn, give them peace with their enemies: peace of mind, peace of heart, and peace in relationships. Peace is a by-product of pleasing Him. Our struggle is not with flesh and blood, but our enemies are the principalities and powers of darkness—our enemy is the devil and his cohorts. Some people picture the devil as a little red guy with horns and a pitch fork. It is important for us to know that the wicked one is all too real and a worthy opponent. We must have a strategy for dealing with him. The Bible mentions satan fifty-five times and it mentions the devil sixty-one times in the New Testament. God is obviously warning us. If you believe there is a God, you must believe there is a devil and he is our enemy. The Lord has given us the authority and the means to subdue the enemy and bring peace to hearts and minds.

## Deliverance

According to the ***American Heritage Dictionary***, *deliverance* may be defined as "rescue from bondage or danger or a publicly expressed opinion or judgment, such as the verdict of a jury." In our pursuit to please our heavenly Father, we can expect His rescue in times of trouble. We can expect the chains of bondage to fall from us. After we repent, we can expect God's verdict on our behalf to always be "not guilty." The writer of Hebrews says, "Let us therefore come boldly to the throne of grace, that we may obtain mercy and find grace to help in time of need" (Hebrews 4:16). He will help us in our time of need.

We also find in Psalm 18:19 that He delivers me because He delights in me. King David messed up time and time again; no one could dare say he was perfect in the sight of the Lord. However, he sings in his song recorded in 2 Samuel 22:20 about God's deliverance being the result of pleasing Him. David pleased God through giving Him his whole heart. Once we give ourselves to Him, God can change us and make us what He needs for us to be .

Continuing in our search, we come to understand how much it means to the Lord when we set our hearts and minds to please Him. Numbers 14:8 says, "If the LORD delight in us, then he will bring us in this land, and give it us; a land which floweth with milk and honey" (KJV). God's promise is to take us to a good place—a blessed place—when we please Him. Provision is readily available in this place and it's sweet to be there.

**Favor**

God is no respecter of persons; however, His heart becomes attracted to our heart as we please Him. God's pleasure brings us His favor and the favor of others. We read about King David discussing God's favor: "Then the king said to Zadok, 'Carry the ark of God back into the city. If I find favor in the eyes of the LORD, He will bring me back and show me both it and His dwelling place'" (2 Samuel 15:25). David hungered for God's favor, but he wanted it so that He could see the Ark and God's dwelling place. God's favor opens up God's dwelling place to us.

Be holy as He is holy. Wickedness will rob you of God's favor. Jeremiah 16:12-13 tells us that the sin of Israel was that they didn't listen to the Lord and they followed after their own desires:

> And you have done worse than your fathers, for behold, each one follows the dictates of his own evil heart, so that no one listens to Me. Therefore I will cast you out of this land into a land that you do not know, neither you nor your fathers; and there you shall serve other gods day and night, where I will not show you favor.

"Favor" is closely related to delight or pleasure. ***Strong's Exhaustive Concordance*** defines "favor" as "to bend or stoop in kindness." In royal courts, subjects want to receive the favor of their king. The Bible encourages us to seek the King of King's favor. King David entreated the Lord's favor with his whole heart (Psalm 119:58) and so should we.

In the last book of the Old Testament, a directive is given, "But now entreat God's favor, That He may be gracious to us" (Malachi 1:9). Under the new covenant, God's grace has already been extended to all who believe on Jesus Christ as their Lord. However, the principle in this verse which directs us to ask earnestly is still valid today. *Entreat* is an action verb; it requires us to seek His heart to cause Him to bend towards us in kindness.

## Seeking God's Heart

The Lord has good thoughts towards us. Just like an earthly father, our heavenly Father wants to give us a hope and a future. He promises us in the book of Jeremiah that as we call on Him, He'll listen to us. When we seek Him, we WILL find Him. It's a promise! All He wants is for us to seek Him with our whole heart. Seeking Him has major benefits. He's telling us to seek Him and then He tells us all the good things He's going to do for us when we do. That's a great deal!

> I will visit you and perform My good word toward you, and cause you to return to this place. For I know the thoughts that I think toward you, says the LORD, thoughts of peace and not of evil, to give you a future and a hope. Then you will call upon Me and go and pray to Me, and I will listen to you. And you will seek Me and find Me, when you search for Me with all your heart. I will be found by you, says the LORD (Jeremiah 29:10-14).

How do we seek His heart? Proverbs 3:3-4 says, "Let not mercy and truth forsake you; Bind them around your neck, Write them on the tablet of your heart, And so find favor and high esteem in the sight of God and man." As we treasure His Word and do it, the Lord will not only favor us, but will hold us in high esteem. We will be valued highly by the Lord. Not only will God notice you, but your peers will notice you and value you.

**ACTION POINT: As you pursue God's heart, you will gain His favor.**

# Chapter 15

# Saved For Good Works

## A Grandfather's Lap

I have a friend who has many grandkids. He loves his grandkids and always enjoys spending time with them. Kids behave like kids and they usually don't hide it from their grandfather when they want that new toy or special gift. However, my friend has one grandchild who will climb up in his lap just to snuggle. That grandchild will say, "Grandpa, I love you soooooo much." There is never an expectation of getting anything in return; that child just shows his unconditional love. That grandson says, "Grandpa, I want to be just like you when I grow up." The motive is pure—expecting only love in return. Grandpa just melts at this adoration and love. He loves all of his grandkids, but this one is special—this one is his favorite. This grandchild has more favor. He would give that child anything he ever wanted; Grandpa would move heaven and earth to bless this child.

This is exactly how the Lord feels. He loves all of His children, but that one who loves Him and has dedicated their heart to Him has his full attention. The worship and love that is shown to the Lord makes us His delight.

## Loving God

The common pursuit of man is love. We want to be loved and we want to love. What in mankind makes us share that desire? Even the humanist psychologist Abraham Maslow recognized that to be a fully functioning human being, you must fulfill the basic need of love—to love and to be loved. There are poems, songs, movies, and plays all exploring this basic human need.

Mankind is made in the image of God. There's a famous corporate saying in advertising today that says, "Image is everything." What does image entail? Our image is our likeness. Genesis 1:26, "God spoke: Let us make human beings in our image, make them reflecting our nature" (MSG). Since man is a reflection of God, our need for love simply reflects His need for love.

God demonstrates His need or desire for love by the Old Testament command—directive—which He issued to Moses: "For if you carefully keep all these commandments which I command you to do—to love the LORD your God, to walk in all His ways, and to hold fast to Him" (Deuteronomy 11:22). Moses further elaborates in Deuteronomy 30:20, "that you may cling to Him, for He is your life and the length of your days..." The Lord wants us to be dependent on Him, and if we are, He won't let us down. He's a rock upon whom we can stand and a tower under whom we may find shelter.

This is not just an old covenant thought; the desire that God has for love was restated in the New Covenant. We read in Matthew 22:37 where Jesus says, "You shall love the LORD your God with all your heart, with all your soul, and with all your mind." God wants us to love Him!! Plain and simple!!

How do we show God that we love Him? Jesus told us that if we love Him, we'll obey the Bible.

> Jesus answered and said to him, "If anyone loves Me, he will keep My word; and My Father will love him, and We will come to him and make Our home with him. He who does not love Me does not keep My words; and the word which you hear is not Mine but the Father's who sent Me (John 14:23-24).

When we love God, there are promises that He makes to us. God is going to take care of us. This promise made in the Old Testament is still valid for us today:

> Because he has set his love upon Me, therefore I will deliver him; I will set him on high, because he has known My name. He shall call upon Me, and I will answer him; I will be with him in trouble; I will deliver him and honor him. With long life I will satisfy him, And show him My salvation. (Psalm 91:14-16).

He promises us deliverance. He'll elevate us. He will honor us and satisfy us with long life. God is so good to us.

## What is Your Motive?

There's one group of people who want to love God and live in His grace. Sometimes these are called the "greasy grace" folks. There's another extreme group of people who want to be keepers of the law: do this... do this... don't do this. Just like in everyday life, there is always a balance that we should strive to maintain. Grace is important, but so is doing the work of Jesus and promoting His Kingdom.

What is your motive in capturing God's heart? Are you looking for a genie in a bottle who will grant your every wish? Are you looking to please your heavenly Father? This entire book is about pleasing God—putting a smile on His face—making Him proud of you. We've explored what that means and how to do it. We've looked at Biblical examples and studied passages in the Word. Our motivating factor in life should be to please the Father—to capture His heart. However, there's a very important fact that we must understand:

**WE ARE NOT SAVED *BY* GOOD WORKS;<br>WE ARE SAVED *FOR* GOOD WORKS.**

We were created for God's good pleasure. The good works we do brings that good pleasure to our heavenly Father. Paul writes to the church at Ephesus, "For we are His workmanship, created in Christ Jesus for good works, which God prepared beforehand that we should walk in them" (Ephesians 2:10). We were created for doing these good works. The grace and power that we need has been given to us in order to be effective. Heaven is not bought with good works, but they do capture our Father's heart.

Adam gave away his legal right in the earth to satan and he became the god of this world (2 Corinthians 4:4). Jesus came into the world to defeat satan in the earth. It is written, "For this purpose the Son of God was manifested, that He might destroy the works of the devil" (1 John 3:8). He came to openly defeat satan and his demon forces and pay the price for the sin of mankind once and for all. When Jesus left the earth, He sent the Holy Spirit to empower Christians to carry His authority. All power was given to the Son of God and then He told the disciples, "All authority has been given to Me in heaven and on earth. Go therefore..." He gave us His authority and power and the Holy Spirit to back it up and now His expectation is for us to continue on doing His works in the earth. Why? Defeating the devil glorifies the Lord.

As Christians, we need to live right. Jesus offers forgiveness when we mess up, but we should still purpose to live right. The point I wish to make is that the motive in doing right things should be to please our heavenly Father—not to get to heaven because you don't get there because of doing right things. Nonetheless, we should still live right—in righteousness—do right things and bring honor to the Father.

My daughter is my daughter and I love her. She is part of my family. When she behaves properly and does things that are right and just, I am very proud. If she should behave improperly, I would love her, but I would be disappointed in her actions and decisions. She honors me or dishonors me by her actions. A child is the reflection of their parents. We, too, are God's reflection in the earth. It is through our actions that our heavenly Father. is either honored or dishonored.

The Bible tells us to imitate God as dear children. It is endearing for Him to see us act like Him. Jesus went about doing good and healing all; His life was filled with good works. We, too, are to go about our everyday lives doing good works.

## Profitable to Man & God

> This is a faithful saying, and these things I want you to affirm constantly, that those who have believed in God should be careful to maintain good works. These things are good and profitable to men (Titus 3:8).

First of all, the verse above is trustworthy. Paul wants to emphasize the stated truth repeatedly—continually—forever. Let it be known that all Christians should be guarded and attentive to persevere in good works—the works of Jesus. If we are admonished to be careful to do them, there must be a natural, earthly pull to stop doing the good works. These works are profitable to both men and God. When you are found pleasing to God, man reaps the temporal benefit and God is glorified. It's a win-win situation.

## Let God Be Glorified

We don't do good works to be seen, but when good works are seen the goal is for God to be glorified. "Let your light so shine before men, that they may see your good works and glorify your Father in heaven" (Matthew 5:16). Our prayer should always be: more of Jesus, less of me.

**ACTION POINT: Let your heart's cry be: more of Jesus, less of me.**

## Our Duty

Roman author of the first century, Gaius Petronius, said: "One good turn deserves another." He knew the value of sowing and reaping. A broad look at this ancient quote can be gleaned. One good deed done by one spurs another to do a good deed, too. It's inspirational to see the good deeds of others. The Apostle Paul wrote in Hebrews 10:24, "And let us consider one another in order to stir up love and good works." Our good works encourage others to do good works. This should be part of our everyday life—at school, work, church, or the grocery store. Let us encourage one another to continue in good works so that the Lord will be glorified.

**ACTION POINT: Let our lives stir others to love God and do good works.**

# Chapter 16

# A Final Word

## Conclusion

We began our journey by finding out that man was created for God's pleasure. As we have walked together through this book, we went back in time to when Lucifer fell to the earth and became the god of this world. In order for God to have legal access back in the earth, His Son was born into the earth through a virgin. Hence, Jesus, the shepherd, came in through the door of the sheepgate.

God wanted a family. He made agreements with man throughout the ages. He searched for those whose hearts were completely His. We explored the covenants between God and man and we ended with the New Covenant. This last Covenant allows for man to be born-again or born anew into the family of God. Luke 10:19 says, "For the Son of Man has come to seek and to save that which was lost." The opportunity for salvation was made available to those who had not yet made that commitment.

Next, we looked and defined *delight* in the Scripture. Christians are exhorted to delight in the Lord, and when we do He will delight in us.

Many things that please the Lord were looked at in depth. In order to gain a full understanding of what He likes, we also looked at things that displease Him. Those who have gone before us were looked at to see what turns the face of the Lord toward one and maybe not the other.

Salvation is by grace; we can do nothing to earn it. Righteousness is by grace; we don't deserve heaven, but Jesus made the way for us. While on this earth, Jesus did good works: raised the dead, healed the sick, and preached the good news. We are not saved BY good works, but we are saved FOR good works. Matthew 7:20 says, "Therefore by their fruits you will know them." Jesus did good works and if we are going to be molded into His image, it is our responsibility and should be our desire to do the good works, too. We do these good works because we want to please God, not to get us into heaven.

Let's continue to move forward in making our Father God proud of us. Our goal should be to always bring pleasure to our God and encourage others to do so, too. As Christians, we can capture God's heart with a right attitude and good works. It is a goal worthy along life's journey to give our all to the Lord.

## My Prayer For You

This is my prayer for you as you continue your life's journey to capture the very heart of God:

> *I pray that you become well acquainted with God's will for your life and that on the way to your destiny you become the likeness of your heavenly Father. I pray that the Holy Spirit flows through you with His awesome power as the Helper and the teacher of the Church. I pray you allow Jesus to be wisdom, righteousness, sanctification, and deliverance in your life (1 Corinthians 1:30). It is my prayer that you walk in the spirit and live a life pleasing to God by becoming like Him and doing good works which glorify God. Amen and amen.*

For this reason we have always prayed for you, ever since we heard about you. We ask God to fill you with the knowledge of his will, with all the wisdom and understanding that his Spirit gives. Then you will be able to live as the Lord wants and will always do what pleases him. Your lives will produce all kinds of good deeds, and you will grow in your knowledge of God.

Colossians 1:9-10, TEV

# About the Author

**Diane Parsons** is a wife, mother, and Bible student. She has earned two Bible School certificates and a Bachelors degree in Business with a major in Accounting. After earning her degree, she began working in the ministry and has done so for over twenty years. She has served in various capacities in church and parachurch organizations.

Diane became a Christian at nineteen and began a life-long study of how to please God. Her analytical and thoughtful style brings insight to Scripture as she focuses on the practical application of Bible truths.

The author lives in Virginia with her husband Darrell and their beautiful daughter Brianna. She currently serves on the staff of international worship leader and teacher, Dr. Ron Kenoly.

## Parsons Publishing House

*Your Voice Your World*™

**AVAILABLE AT YOUR LOCAL BOOKSTORE**

**P.O. Box 488, Stafford VA 22554 USA**

**www.ParsonsPublishingHouse.com**

**Email: info@ParsonsPublishingHouse.com**

---

### THE EFFECTIVE PRAISE & WORSHIP LEADER
### by Dr. Ron Kenoly

What is a good worship leader? What does a pastor want in a worship leader? Use this book as a measuring stick for the anointed person you want to become. From his vast experience, Ron Kenoly shares insight into the office of the worship leader. Order today for only $10.95.

### The PRIORITY OF PRAISE & WORSHIP
### by Dr. Ron Kenoly

Ron Kenoly has stepped into a new season of ministry to mentor worship leaders, pastors and worshipers. Through this book, you will receive proven answers to common and uncommon issues from one of the nation's most anointed and experienced worship leading authorities. Each chapter is designed to take you to a higher level of excellence in your worship experience. Order your copy today for only $12.95.

## WITH EVERY BEAT OF MY HEART
## A Weekly Devotional by Jeff North

Explore real life examples in real Christian living. ***With Every Beat of My Heart*** takes the reader to a place where inspirational stories and poems stay upon their hearts and lips throughout the day. This book offers a practical message with a godly foundation to encourage, motivate, and bring comfort (224 pages). Order today for only $14.95.

## PORTRAIT OF A PASTOR'S HEART
## A Manual on Caring for the Sheep
## by Bishop Gerald Doggett

This book is a must for pastors, elders, students & laymen who want to learn to care for the flock of God. Bishop Gerald Doggett paints a rare and intimate portrait of a pastor's heart. He covers TOPICS such as: Spirit of a Finisher, The Necessity of the Divine Call and A Beautiful Portrait of Preparation. Order your copy today for only $12.95.

## RELEASE YOUR WORDS - IMPACT YOUR WORLD
## by Darrell Parsons

Your words can make a difference! God has done something in the life of every believer. He has placed treasures inside you that He wants to use to touch hearts and minds. In this book, Darrell Parsons challenges you to use your voice to impact the world around you today. Order your copy for only $9.95.

## MOUNTAIN VIEW - A Photo Collection
## by Doris Beets

Contained in these pages is a beautiful, color pictorial discovery of a community in East Tennesseee where splendor is exemplified and where beauty is personified. In this book, Doris Beets attempts to give you a glimpse of the world that captured her heart over 75 years ago. Only $29.95.

## LIFTING HIM UP
## by Ron Kenoly & Dick Bernal

Worship leader Ron Kenoly teams up with his pastor, Dick Bernal, in this practical guide to praise and worship. You'll learn how to enter into the Lord's presence, plus you'll gain insight into the scriptural role of praise and worship in your life and church. Order your copy today for only $12.95.

## SILENCING THE ENEMY WITH PRAISE
## by Robert Gay

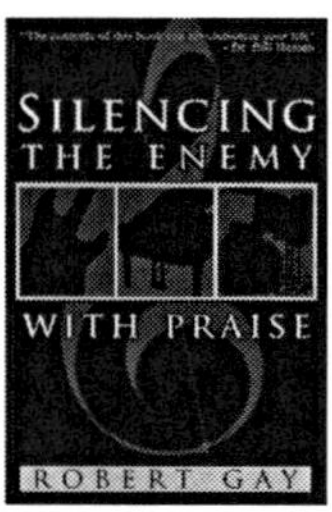


Praise is a weapon used to command the enemies in your life to be silent. Robert Gay is known around the world as the father of warfare praise in the Kingdom. In this book, he expands on the Bible truth of praise and how God wants to use praise in your life. Only $11.95.

## 30 DAYS TO A BETTER PRAYER LIFE
### by Nora King

In this exciting book, Nora King offers a fresh look at prayer. In only thirty days, you can improve the effectiveness of your personal prayer life by utilizing the daily truths given. You will learn about Genuine Prayer, United Prayer, Dare to Pray, and many more. Only $11.95.

## MEMOIR TO MY BOSOM BUDDY
### by Janet Bergdoll

Within a two-week period, both Janet and her sister were diagnosed with breast cancer. As mother, wife and registered nurse, she began treatment by the book. Soon, however, her journey called out for a therapy under her control; she began journaling through her diagnosis, treatment and recovery. This inspirational book is about her walk with breast cancer. Only $12.95.

**AVAILABLE AT YOUR LOCAL BOOKSTORE**

Breinigsville, PA USA
10 September 2010

245127BV00005B/3/P

9 781602 730083